The Art of Becoming a WHOLE PERSON

The Art of Becoming a WHOLE PERSON

Cecil G. Osborne

WORD BOOKS
PUBLISHER
4800 WEST WACO DRIVE
WACO, TEXAS
76703

124405

Printed in the United States of America
ISBN 0-8499-0075-1
Library of Congress catalog card number: 77-92465

Contents

Preface

In his highly interesting book, *How Come It's Taking Me So Long To Get Better?* [1] Lane Adams writes, "I shrink when I think of the times I have mounted the pulpit, recited the conversion experience of the Apostle Paul, and then indicated that he went out and turned the world upside down for Jesus *immediately*. This simply was not the case. . . . "

The author then deals with the generally accepted fact that something like *eighteen* years elapsed between Paul's conversion and the beginning of his missionary journeys—three years in Damascus and the Arabian desert, fourteen years in Tarsus, and a year in Antioch during which he made his second visit to Jerusalem.

It is comforting, when discouraged over one's pathetically slow or erratic progress in spiritual and emotional growth, to remember Paul's eighteen years of preparation, to read his astonishing lament years later, "I know I am rotten through and through so far as my old sinful nature is concerned, . . . " [2] and to recall that long after he had been preaching the gospel far and wide he referred to himself as "foremost among sinners." [3]

The impatient human mind longs for quick and easy answers to complex problems. We never fully outgrow the instinctual childhood love of magic. No matter how mature one may be, there still lurks within the hidden recesses of the personality the age-old longing for an easier, more expeditious, less painful solution of life's complexities.

New panaceas and fresh methodologies are being constantly promoted as "newer and better." Theologians, with predictable regularity, rethink their theological stance. Some of the new methods and approaches have much to offer, and many old movements with a new vocabulary produce some gratifying results. In recent years Transcendental Meditation (proponents and detractors still argue its merits or evils), Transactional Analysis (TA), Esalen, est (Erhard Seminar Training), the Lay Witness Movement, the charismatic movement, Faith at Work, Yokefellows, Primal Therapy, encounter groups, and half a hundred other movements and esoteric approaches have been offered as a means of spiritual growth. The claims of some of these and other movements are discussed in the final chapters.

I find it comforting to remind myself that the Twelve who walked with Jesus did not become spiritual giants over night. One

betrayed him, one denied him, one doubted him, and all fled in
terror of their lives at the end.

Were these men "whole"? The truth is that we know very little
about them. Of the Twelve, six are not recorded as having uttered
a word. Of the remaining six, three came forth with single utter-
ances of no great profundity such as, "Where in this lonely place
can we find bread enough to feed such a crowd?" [4] And of the three
comprising the inner circle—Peter, James and John—two wanted
to burn down a village which had offended them, and Peter proved
a moral weakling at the end.[5]

This fact is pointed out, not to deprecate the Twelve, but in
order to emphasize an inescapable fact: growth can be a painfully
slow process.

The Bible is a realistic book. It doesn't gloss over the defects of
its characters. We learn that there was drunkenness in the com-
munion service at Corinth, as well as blatant immorality, "and of
a kind that is not even found among pagans; for a man is living
with his father's wife." [6] Then there is Paul's own admission of a
crushing depression so severe that he despaired of life.[7] There was
"bitterness and wrath and anger and clamor and slander . . .
with . . . malice," [8] among the Christians at Ephesus.

Frequent references are made to the great spiritual power of the
first-century Christians; but candor compels us to face the fact that
even these dynamic believers suffered in many instances from
serious sins of both the spirit and the flesh.

This book is an eclectic [9] approach to wholeness. Just as in medicine there is no one broad spectrum drug which will cure all
diseases, so in the realm of the spirit and personality there is no
single approach or technique which will meet the specific needs
of every person. We humans are all incredibly different, with
unique needs, and we are at various stages of growth and development.

I once conducted a retreat in a church of over eight thousand
members. Instead of the cold, impersonal atmosphere one expects to
find in a huge church, I discovered an amazing warmth. They had
a kind of cafeteria-type approach to growth. There were groups for
young mothers, senior citizens, young married couples, middle-aged
people, a fantastic youth program, interest groups, Yokefellow
groups, and dozens of other varied activities to appeal to any age
or interest. It was a multi-faceted church, meeting the unique needs
of people at the various stages of their growth. And what a dynamic
church it was! The atmosphere was one of love and joy. The people
were warm and friendly and outgoing. They embraced each other
spontaneously. One of the ministers attributed the church's dy-

namism and love to the large number of small face-to-face groups operating in the church. Theirs was a truly eclectic approach.

I like to visualize Jesus, the only supremely whole individual in history, at the center of an immense circle whose outer circumference encloses all humanity. Each person in this vast throng must find his or her own path to the one who is the Way, the Truth and the Life. There is *no one way* to him; no one true church, nor any single method, movement or creed which is the "best" for everyone. Perhaps the most effective way to achieve wholeness is to choose whatever approach appeals to one spiritually, emotionally, aesthetically, and intellectually.

This book is a study of the factors which have made us less than whole, and a presentation of some approaches and movements which make for wholeness, integration, spiritual and emotional well-being.

Robert Louis Stevenson once said, "I hate to write but I love to have written." Somewhat in the same vein I can say that for me writing is hard work, but the study of the factors which can make one a whole person has been a thrilling and heartening enterprise. It is my hope and prayer that you will find something in these pages that will encourage you in your journey toward wholeness.

1

Are You a Whole Person?

> "God offers to every man the choice
> between truth and repose. Take which
> you please; you can never have both."
> —Ralph Waldo Emerson

Fred, about thirty-five years old, wore the tense, worried look of a man who is doubleparked, overdrawn at the bank, and late for an appointment. He seated himself abstractedly in my office, totally unaware of his surroundings.

"I have a feeling," he said, "that there's this great big union that everyone in the world belongs to but me, and I don't even know where to sign up as an apprentice. I always feel as if I were on the outside looking in; an observer, but never a participant in life." He smiled a little, deprecatingly, but the wan smile could not conceal his look of bleak hopelessness and loneliness. I asked about his early childhood.

"Well, my father was a very angry, bitter, unforgiving man. When he died, not a soul at the funeral shed a tear. I think we were all secretly glad he was gone." He went on to describe his childhood in an unloving home, and the various factors which had rendered him unable to give or receive love. His marriage was intact, he had a fairly good job, and other external factors were reasonably satisfactory, but he carried a burden of sadness and loneliness that cried out for a solution. Fred functioned normally in society, but he was not a whole person. His capacity for happiness and fulfillment was severely limited, because he was never loved as a child, and consequently found himself unable to respond normally to love and acceptance as an adult. His enormous reservoir of diffused anxiety rendered him unable to enjoy life.

It is easy to diagnose Fred's symptoms. He has an anxiety neurosis, and is suffering from depression. Friends or relatives, in a misguided and futile effort to help, had offered him such useless advice as:

11

"Try not to worry."
"You shouldn't feel that way. Count your blessings."
"Look on the bright side."
"Just put those thoughts out of your mind."
"Pray and read your Bible."
"Think of all the people who are worse off than you."
"You must try harder to relax."

His efforts to apply those bromides only made him feel more guilty and depressed.

Apologizing for Living

Tanya, a woman approaching fifty and looking thirty-six, with a dry, sardonic sense of humor and a sad, depressed voice, was having dinner with my wife and me at a restaurant. During the course of the meal she thanked the waiter profusely half-a-dozen times for such expected services as handing her a menu or bringing a glass of water. I said, facetiously, "Tanya, I'd like to suggest an inscription for your tombstone. It should read, 'Thank you, thank you, thank you so much.'" She smiled faintly and said, "No, I already have my own inscription in mind. It will read, 'I'm sorry to put you to so much trouble. Please forgive me. It's all my fault. I'm very sorry.'"

I knew why Tanya felt such a need to apologize for living, for I had listened to her in scores of hours of Primal Integration, as she, regressed to childhood, relived the trauma of those early years. Until age eleven she had cried herself to sleep very night. Her cold and unfeeling parents had never held or cuddled her, never affirmed her in any way. On the contrary, they told her a thousand times that she was a bother, a burden, and unlike other children. As a child she didn't know why she felt so miserable by day and so terrified at night. In her primal sessions as she wept seemingly endless tears, she began to get in touch with normal human emotions, all of which had been buried beneath a vast reservoir of childhood hurts. Until she began the process, she had been incapable of love, anger, aspiration, joy, sadness or any other basic emotion. The life-long depression which she had come to accept as normal is not an emotion, but rather the shutting off of all emotions. Unconsciously she feared to feel lest she reexperience the innumerable hurts of childhood.

Tanya is liked by everyone who knows her. She is agreeable, pleasant, witty in her sardonic way, and can afford any luxury her heart desires. But the results of a psychological test she took revealed that in terms of self-acceptance she scored zero. She is not a whole person. The enormous damage done to her by rejecting parents made it virtually impossible for her to enjoy any aspect of life. She had joined a church at one time, hoping that this would somehow give her a reason for living. Nothing changed, though she gave her best to the effort.

At last she has a goal in life: to become a whole person. Nothing matters to her but this; and through Primal Integration she is gradually being released from the encapsulated pain which has kept her from being a feeling, loving individual.

Some Are More Whole by Nature

Some people seem to be better integrated, more whole, more "together" by nature, than others of us are by grace and hard work. Joe and Elaine are a case in point. They are a charming, good-looking young couple. In their first counseling session Joe said grimly that he wanted out of the marriage. His wife, he explained, was a screamer, as her entire family had been. He had come from a quiet family and had no intention of staying married to an explosive, screaming wife for the rest of his life.

Elaine had no complaints except that she would have liked Joe to be more tolerant of her angry outbursts. I saw her alone a week later, and laid it out gently but firmly: "If you can't control your screaming, you'll lose him permanently. You may have already. I know of few men who will put up with that sort of thing. I realize it's a life-long habit, and it may be difficult to control, but you must make an effort. Stop your screaming. Control those outbursts, lower your voice. Blink your eyes three times before you say *anything,* then rephrase the statement so that it's tactful." We spent an hour on that simple formula. I had little hope that a young woman reared in a family of screamers could learn to control her emotions without a vast deal of practice and encouragement. I was wrong.

When they came in together for their next appointment, Joe was relaxed and smiling. Elaine looked smug. "Things are great," Joe began. "She's been just perfect ever since her last visit here." Elaine said that she remembered the formula, to blink three times before speaking and to rephrase everything so that it would sound acceptable. I wondered just how long she could keep this up and asked them to come in a month later to report. They did, and both said that everything was just wonderful. Curious, I asked, "What kind of love did you each receive as children?" They had both been greatly loved, as it turned out. Elaine's parents, though very loud and vocal, gave her consistent, unconditional love. Joe's quiet parents gave him understanding, love and gentleness. Neither could find the slightest reason to criticize their parents.

So, here was the answer. These two delightful young people were able to profit from a simple set of instructions because they were both basically whole persons. They had not been damaged in childhood by parents or other factors. Unconditional, or at least consistent, parental love produces children who can achieve wholeness more easily.

The tremendous importance of the first five years of a child's life was underscored by Leo Tolstoi long before modern psychologists had verified it. He wrote, "From the child of five to myself is but a step; but from the newborn baby to the child of five is an appalling distance." [1] Those who had parents who gave them love in a form the child could accept, and who received consistent discipline backed by warm acceptance, were *fortunate* indeed. For them the process of growing toward wholeness is vastly simplified. Such persons often find it difficult to understand why others cannot make the same progress or mature as quickly as they.

Grace Is Conferred, Wholeness Is Achieved

On the assumption that God's love and grace are conferred, but growth is achieved by our own efforts, I have compiled a set of goals which, though I were to live to be as old as Methuselah, I could never reach fully. Yet, one must be lured toward spiritual and emotional maturity by goals high enough to be challenging, knowing at the same time that failure to reach them all does not condemn one. Here is my list, subject to changes as growth imparts greater wisdom:

1. To possess humility without being aware of it.
2. To love God consistently without feeling religious.
3. To do good in secret without hoping it will be discovered by accident.
4. To listen to the problems of others with concern, and to their good fortune without envy.
5. To accept praise without vanity, and criticism without defensiveness.
6. To be able to enjoy prosperity without pride or guilt, or poverty without complaint.
7. To live as if each day were the last, while planning for the future.
8. To possess integrity without becoming legalistic.
9. To give and receive love, without fear or guilt.
10. To tolerate reasonable stress without complaint.
11. To enjoy both solitude, and the company of others.
12. To be gentle and patient with the young, compassionate with the elderly, and tolerant of the weak and foolish, since I will some day have been all of these.
13. To sin less and less, and confess more and more.

14. To view myself, and others, with amused, friendly, tolerance.
15. To possess self-control without being rigid or intolerant of those who have less of this trait than I.
16. To admit when I am wrong, which is very often.
17. To handle anger constructively.
18. To forgive myself and others readily.
19. To recognize God as the source of all, and to be continually grateful.
20. To be as patient with myself and others, as God is patient with me.
21. To possess the capacity for assertiveness when appropriate.
22. To compete with my previous best, rather than with others; setting goals high enough to be challenging, low enough to be attainable.
23. To have tact without weakness, and strength with gentleness.
24. To love God for himself alone.
25. To face death without regret or fear, knowing that the human caterpillar will become a liberated butterfly in a more glorious dimension of time and space.

One might extend the list indefinitely. No two persons would name identical virtues, but surely in a lengthened list one would want to include a lively sense of humor, without which no one is entirely complete or whole; and one thinks also of the capacity for compassion, the ability to experience reverence and wonder, a love of beauty, and perhaps a hundred other qualities which strike one as admirable.

But compiling a list of desirable attributes is very simple compared to the difficulty of achieving these qualities.

Saints with Tilted Halos

The Bible, with ruthless honesty, depicts its spiritual giants not only in their moments of grandeur, but with all their deficiencies.

There was Simon Peter who had to live not only with the memory of his miserable denial, but also the knowledge that he had been harboring—even after Pentecost—a monumental prejudice against Gentiles.[2] Abraham lied at least on two occasions;[3] Moses, for all his patience, once grew very angry[4]—and one wonders why, in fact, he hadn't abandoned the entire project long before, with all the grumbling and moaning of his rebellious horde. Elijah once fled for his life and went into deep depression,[5] and Solomon, despite his vast wisdom, married a wide assortment of pagan wives and built temples for them, in open violation of divine command.[6] History is replete with accounts of men and women of great spiritual and intellectual power who, in their weaker moments, succumbed to temptation.

Turning to the more recent past, contemplate the magnificent figure of Thomas Jefferson, architect and draftsman of the Declaration of Independence, Ambassador to France, Secretary of State under Washington, and twice president of his country. Of him it was said that he knew something about everything and everything about some things. "You can never be in this man's company," wrote John Quincy Adams in his diary, "without sensing something of the marvelous." But Jefferson was all too human. Biographers tell of the storm of controversy and criticism which raged about him concerning his relationship with two women—Maria Cosway, wife of a British painter, and Sally Heming, a slave girl at his Monticello home. "In his relationship with women," writes historian Max Lerner, "Jefferson seems to have been attracted to the difficult and the forbidden. He was trapped in an age, a class, and a society where miscegenation was practiced but severely punished when made public. He couldn't have escaped a feeling of guilt about this relationship, as suggested by his long history of migraine headaches. This doesn't negate my view of him as a whole man, although a complex and guilt-ridden one." [7]

While the discovery that the great and notable have been less than perfect does not lessen our own guilt in the same or other areas, it can give us a more balanced view of our humanity. It underscores the lament of Isaiah:

> All we like sheep have gone astray,
>   we have turned everyone to his own way;
> and the Lord has laid on him
>   the iniquity of us all. [8]

What Is Wholeness?

Who is whole? And what is wholeness? We can define it, to begin with, in terms of what it is not. Wholeness does not imply moral or spiritual perfection. It is not a synonym for complete serenity, or euphoria, or a state of perpetual bliss or contentment. It is not total fulfillment, though one who is whole stands a far better chance of being fulfilled.

The words *wholeness* and *holiness* come from the same root. *Holy* is derived from the Anglo Saxon term *halig,* meaning to be healthy. Our word *whole* comes from the Anglo Saxon word *hal,* meaning completeness, or integration. Wholeness does not mean perfection, nor holiness as ordinarily understood, but does imply being healthy in mind, body and spirit, and having healthy relationships and attitudes.

Some tend to believe that we grow into wholeness, or maturity, as we age. Would that this were true! Age does very little for us as personalities except to make us "more so." The crotchety usually become more crotchety, the critical become more critical, the loving and forgiving become more beautifully so. We do not achieve emotional maturity simply by putting in our time on this planet.

Some of our more youthful illusions perish, or give way to more mature concepts, if we are in the process of becoming whole persons. A psychologist friend of mine, a fine Christian, said thoughtfully one day, "You know, I'm rather disappointed. I have a good practice, a fine income, a $100,000 home with a pool, two cars, fine kids, good health and a great wife—but somehow I'm not all that happy. I thought that when I reached this point in life I'd be happier than I am. There has to be something more. I seem to be vaguely discontented."

It is my belief that there is a God-inspired discontent within us which keeps us feeling unfulfilled and lures us on toward a higher degree of wholeness. God keeps us seeking, searching, growing, until we finally discover the ultimate—which, I am sure, will not be attained in this one lifetime. Surely the search must go on through the endless reaches of time.

Granting that any wholeness we attain here will be relative rather than ultimate, we can define a whole person as one who lives by recognized moral standards and is happy to do so; is not in rebellion against rules and regulations established by God or society. The immature, impatient, hostile revolutionary wants to make society over *immediately,* unaware of the fact that important social changes normally require considerable time.

A whole person acquires patience with himself, with others, and with life, and does not expect to receive unconditional love and acceptance *all* the time. One who is growing toward maturity and wholeness develops a tolerance for frustration. Unlike the young child, or an alcoholic, whose capacity for frustration is poorly developed, the integrated, maturing individual learns to tolerate disappointment, delay, and occasional failure.

Growth toward wholeness involves learning to give. Most people are familiar with the statement of Jesus that "It is more blessed to give than to receive." [9] It is not generally recognized, however, that it is also more *therapeutic* to give than to receive. When we give—whether it is love, or money, or encouragement or time—we discover that the very act of giving is a therapeutic (healing) factor in our own personalities, as well as in relationships. It speeds our growth toward maturity.

A Whole Person Is Involved

Comedian Flip Wilson once said, "Religiously I am a Jehovah's

Bystander. They wanted me to be a Witness, but I didn't want to get involved." His not-so-subtle sideswipe at the impersonal people who don't wish to become involved in the problems of the world points up the fact that giving is a way of getting involved with others. I live in a suburb near San Francisco where, as in most large cities, muggings and purse snatchings are increasing at an alarming rate. Newspapers reported the case of an elderly woman walking in a high-risk area of the city who was knocked down and robbed by a young hoodlum. She screamed, and a man started chasing the mugger, yelling as he did so. Others joined the chase, and the young man was caught within a block by an angry group of about twenty persons. The mugger was finally rescued from the mob by the police, who hustled him away to jail. Those people *really* got involved! And what satisfaction it must have given them.

When we become involved in the lives and fortunes of others we become vulnerable, just as any relationship subjects one to that risk. One young man whom I helped after he was paroled from San Quentin prison made a magnificent success of his life. A second one, for whom I helped provide a job, a car, and total acceptance by a church group, robbed the church, took off with the car, and wrote me from a Florida prison three months later. Of *course* there is a risk! Lend money and it may not be returned. Help an accident victim and you may have to go to court as a witness. The person helped may be ungrateful. Friendship offered may be betrayed.

Does this risk mean we are to become the naïve victims of rip-off artists, lending money without deliberation, helping any and all on their own terms? Not at all. Each of us has a given amount of love, money, time, energy or influence which can be shared with others. There is a limit to what we can do; therefore, consecrated common sense would indicate that we are to help people *on our own terms,* not on theirs. The alcoholic who asks you to pay for food and a night's lodging actually needs something more difficult to give— a ride to an alcoholic rehabilitation center, or the equivalent. The emotionally immature individual who will not live within his income and lives off money borrowed from friends and relatives is not a fit subject for a loan which will only perpetuate his dependence and financial instability. Give on *your* terms, whether it is money, love or energy. It took me many years to learn this fact. A compassionate, overcompliant individual can give an enormous proportion of his time and resources without accomplishing much. In encouraging us to "give to him who begs from you, and do not refuse him who would borrow from you," [10] Jesus is not suggesting an abdication of common sense and mature judgment. He did not accede to every request. He gave of himself where it would accomplish the most good.

Becoming involved in a cause greater than yourself can provide a means of growth toward wholeness. There are thousands of worthy causes in need of assistance. The world is hurting in innumerable ways, but it is important to find the precise sphere where your energies will produce the most results. I once had a friend whose limitless compassion outstripped his judgment. His concerns were global in extent. At one point he flew with a group of friends to Washington, D.C., in an effort to dissuade the president from some course of action they deemed foolhardy. They failed to secure an audience with the president. For the next twenty years I observed his efforts to solve international and national problems through oratory, petitions, and any means at his command. He was certain that he always knew not only the solution to this or that international crisis, but he could also place the blame where it belonged. He always knew which nation and what leader was responsible. In the course of time my friend, finding his crusades rather unfruitful, ceased trying to solve national and international problems and busied himself with individuals where, so far as I could see, he made a genuine contribution.

Who's to Blame?

A man went to visit an acquaintance. As he entered the door a large dog accompanied him. In the first five minutes the dog managed to upset an end table and a lamp, misbehaved on an expensive oriental rug, then stretched out on the sofa with his muddy feet. The visitor seemed oblivious to the damage being done by the dog. Finally, with ill-concealed exasperation, the host said, "I'm sorry, but you'll just have to put your dog out." The visitor said in considerable astonishment, "*My* dog! I thought it was *yours!*" As we consider the malfunctioning society in which we live, beset with a host of problems ranging from poverty to threat of atomic holocaust, there is a natural tendency to ask, "Whose dog is it?" "Who is to blame? Who is responsible for all of the sin, suffering and sorrow in the world? Is it the corporate guilt of society? Shall we blame the president, the congress, the home, the school system, organized religion?"

This instinctual need to find the culprit must always end in failure. No one is to blame; everyone is. We are all part of a faulty system, and each of us is marred in the making, thus faulty in performance.

We cannot save the world, but we can reach out in love and concern to individuals. I am not responsible for solving the world's problems, but I am responsible to become a whole person in so far as I am able; and this wholeness implies automatically that I will feel concern for others.

If growth is the meaning of life, as I think it probably is, then the goal for each of us is to grow toward the ultimate—wholeness. To the degree that we can become whole, integrated, complete, unified, we will reach out in love and concern.

Spiritual growth need not take the form of an all-out, anxiety-producing, guiltridden, humorless, exhausting campaign. On the contrary, it is well to remember that Jesus took time out for social events. There was the wedding in Cana, and weddings in that part of the world were gala affairs. He was accused by his enemies of being a wine bibber and a glutton, an exaggeration of his tendency to attend dinners and banquets.

Nadine Stair of Louisville, Kentucky, was eighty-five years old when she wrote this:

If I Had My Life to Live Over Again

I'd dare to make more mistakes next time. I'd relax. I would be sillier than I have been this trip. I would take fewer things seriously. I would take more chances. I would take more trips. I would climb more mountains and swim more rivers. I would eat more ice cream and fewer beans. I would perhaps have more actual troubles, but I'd have fewer imaginary ones.

You see, I'm one of those people who live sensibly and sanely hour after hour, day after day. Oh, I've had my moments, and if I had to do it over again I'd have more of them. In fact, I'd try to have nothing else. Just moments, one after another, instead of living so many years ahead of each day. I've been one of those persons who never goes anywhere without a thermometer, a hot water bottle, a raincoat and a parachute. If I had to do it again, I'd travel lighter.

If I had my life to live over, I would start barefoot earlier in the spring and stay that way later in the fall. I would go to more dances. I would ride more merry-go-rounds. I would pick more daisies.[11]

When my wife and I eat out she sometimes asks me to order for her, for I know her likes and dislikes rather well—no coffee, and no dessert; roquefort dressing, and so on. But if I were dining with a stranger I would not think of presuming to order for him, being unaware of his tastes and preferences. In the same vein, rather than making specific suggestions about how you can achieve a greater degree of wholeness, I am offering a menu of principles which have proven beneficial to many people. You will want to make your own selection, to suit your own unique personality, at this particular point in your own emotional and spiritual growth.

In succeeding chapters we will deal with some biblical and psychological principles, which can form the basis for your own continued personal growth toward wholeness.

2

Wholeness and Childhood

"He who knows others is wise; He who
knows himself is enlightened."
—The Tao Te Ching

What is it that seemingly predisposes many humans toward neurosis rather than toward wholeness? What are the factors which prevent us from becoming—naturally and easily—mature, loving, accepting persons? How did we get this way?

This chapter, dealing with the sources of malfunctioning personalities, may help rid you of some of your false guilt—if you have any—based on the supposition that you alone are responsible for all of the defects in your personality. In tracing our difficulties to their source—our parents, teachers and other authority figures—we are not seeking to place blame. Rather we are trying to place responsibility where it belongs but *without blame.* Our parents did their best, as did their parents before them. Their failure is the failure of society, the corporate guilt of mankind.

Psychologist Richard Farson, father of five, stated in an interview: "Being a good parent isn't just difficult, it is impossible. There is simply no way to be a good parent in a society organized against children. The best things that happen between parents and children happen by accident or by surprise, breaking all rules. Anyone who isn't bewildered by child-rearing and doesn't find it an extremely formidable and trying experience probably isn't a parent." [1]

Most parents do experience frustration in rearing their children. As children we, too, were frustrated. Can you remember the ten thousand criticisms, and the relatively few fragments of praise? Do you recall the spankings, the verbal abuse, the interminable lectures, the subtle ridicule, the demands to fetch and carry, the accusations of ingratitude and disloyalty when you rebelled?

"If an employer treated his workers in this fashion he would be picketed, boycotted, and brought before the Labor Relations Board.

21

His employees would be sick with loathing and the urge for revenge. Our current discrimination against minority groups is about the only adult parallel in our society for the unkindness imposed upon children." [2]

Not everyone recalls this type of treatment, but I have learned neither to believe nor disbelieve adult claims of a happy, untroubled childhood. I have spent over forty-five years in counseling, and several thousand hours listening to people in Primal Integration Therapy dealing with primal feelings. In this type of therapy the subject lies on a foam rubber mat in a dimly lit room, and is led back into early childhood to relive forgotten or partially buried experiences of infancy and childhood. These buried memories are relived with as much intensity as the original event, and are often expressed with tears, screams, rage, fear, or pleadings. It is a common occurrence for the person having relived a deep and traumatic experience to say, "Good grief, I had no idea all that was down there! I had completely buried those memories and feelings!"

A woman in her forties, who had spent six years with a psychiatrist seeking the basis for her enormous and inexplicable anxiety, finally was taken by her psychiatrist to a hospital and given sodium amytol, the so-called truth serum. Even with the aid of the drug, she was unable or unwilling to divulge her secret. In her third Primal Integration session, with her mind on a split screen, talking to me with one part of her mind and experiencing her childhood with the other portion, she relived the totally repressed memory of being raped—by her own father. It came out slowly, little by little, hour after hour. Later, listening to the taped recording of her sessions, she said, "I couldn't believe that was happening. He wouldn't do a thing like that; but now, listening to that recording, I know it's true."

How Children Are Damaged

In less traumatic ways parents damage their children. They "marshall the age-old devices; they shame, they ignore, they snipe at deviations with a thousand psychic devices. They will not admit their intent to themselves—to kill the judgment and the will of the child where it deviates from their own. But to some extent every parent subconsciously seeks his own immortality, wants the child to be a carbon copy of himself, neurotic or healthy, and he signals this intention to the child in a thousand ways." [3]

A wise high school teacher gave this admonition regarding teenagers: "Treat them like adults, but don't expect them to act that way." If children were to be treated by their parents with as much respect and tact and consideration as adults display to their adult friends, the problem of child-rearing would be immeasurably lessened.

No one maintains that it is easy to rear children. The father of four teenagers said that "There's nothing wrong with teenagers that reasoning with them won't aggravate." A high school teacher once spoke of the "cautious, impenetrable, watchfulness of teenagers, masking their secret contempt of the idiosyncrasies of their incomprehensible elders, with their Stone Age mentality." Someone asked the mother of six very active children how she managed to maintain her serene, placid demeanor. She replied, smiling broadly, "We have a large house, and I hide a lot." Many harrassed mothers must have wished for a larger home, with a place to hide, or some way to escape occasionally from the legitimate but endless demands of their children. It is my firm belief that every mother of small children should have a full day off every week. Children, too, would benefit from a more relaxed, calm mother. The father of five youngsters said, "Insanity is contagious. You can catch it from your kids!"

Confused and frustrated parents often ask what they can say or do, what methods they can employ, to achieve the desired results with their children. I reply, in effect, that while there are some specific guidelines and techniques which can be used to improve parent-child relationships, the most effective approach is for the parents to become mature, whole persons. Often it is not the child who needs counseling, but the parents. Neurotic parents tend to produce damaged children.

The parents are worried about their daughter's obesity; she is depressed because she has no friends. The parents are deeply concerned over their son's bed wetting; he is troubled because his perfectionist parents make unreasonable demands or quarrel incessantly. Mother and father are concerned over their child's poor grades. The youngster has things on his mind which he cannot share with them, lest he receive an interminable lecture. He knows inwardly that they could never understand his private misery, which he senses must be his own fault, for he seems to be to blame for everything else.

The parents are angry and ashamed because their child has stolen something, but he is unable to tell them that he took a substitute for love, because he doesn't know why he stole something he didn't need. Parents take their stuttering child to a speech therapist, but the boy (few girls stutter) cannot tell anyone that he stutters because of repressed anger so deeply buried even he does not know it is there. Usually it is the parents who need the therapy in each of these instances, not the child. It is not that they do not love their child or that they are neurotic (though they may be), but that they do not know some of the fundamentals of child-rearing. A license is required before one may drive a car. Hairdressers take training and are licensed; but any man and woman can have children, though they may not know the slightest thing about child-rearing.

In Primal Integration sessions Sherrilyn was regressed back to childhood and did nothing but weep hysterically for ten, two-hour sessions. She was reliving the childhood experience of having been shifted from school to school when the family moved, finding it difficult to make friends, eating her lunch in the restroom to avoid the rejection she expected in the lunchroom, feigning sickness day after day to escape the horror of facing hostile children who ridiculed her. She dared not tell her parents, for once when she tried to share with them some of her feelings, she received a lecture lasting until midnight. There was no validating of her feelings, no effort to understand her terrifying feelings of rejection and loneliness. The parents were not evil people, just standard, inept, uninformed parents like millions of others.

An Age-old Problem

The problem of parent-child relationships is nothing new. Twenty-five hundred years ago Socrates said, "Our youth now love luxury. They have bad manners, contempt for authority; they show disrespect for their elders. They love to chatter in place of exercise. They no longer rise when elders enter the room. They contradict their parents, babble before company, gobble up their food and tyrannize their teachers." There has never been a time when it was easy for either parent or child.

The problem of permissiveness versus an authoritarian approach on the part of parents is one which is not easily resolved. Kathy, a young married woman, in a primal session was reliving a portion of her traumatic early childhood. Experiencing it with unbelievable intensity, she screamed at her father, "Tell me *no!* Don't let me have everything I ask for. That's *stupid!*" Later she said, "I was experiencing the frustration of knowing that he should have set reasonable limits, but another part of me wanted my own way all the time. He was no help at all."

Erma Bombeck, writing in the Chicago *Sun-Times,* deals with the setting of limits:

" 'You don't love me!' How many times have your kids laid that one on you? And how many times have you, as a parent, resisted the urge to tell them how much?

"Some day when my children are old enough to understand the logic that motivates a mother, I'll tell them.

"I loved you enough to bug you about where you were going, with whom, and what time you would get home.

"I loved you enough to be silent and let you discover your hand-picked friend was a creep.

"I loved you enough to make you return a Milky Way with a bite out of it to a drugstore and confess, 'I stole this.'

"I loved you enough to stand over you for two hours while you cleaned your bedroom, a job that would have taken me fifteen minutes.

"I loved you enough not to make excuses for your lack of respect or your bad manners.

"I loved you enough to ignore 'what every other mother did.'

"I loved you enough to figure you would lie about the party being chaperoned but forgave you for it . . . after discovering I was right.

"I loved you enough to let you stumble, fall, and fail, so that you could learn to stand alone.

"I loved you enough to accept you for what you are, not what I wanted you to be.

"But most of all I loved you enough to say no when you hated me for it. That was the hardest part of all."

Geniuses Were Not All "A" Students

One area of faulty child-rearing which damages many children is an unreasoning and unreasonable emphasis upon good grades. Obviously a child should be encouraged to do his or her best, but this often takes the form of placing undue emphasis upon grades to the exclusion of other factors. Good grades do not automatically guarantee success in later life, nor is poor scholastic performance always followed by failure. "Success is not always the result of a child getting an *A* report card in school," claims Dr. Ronald S. Illingworth, professor of child health at the University of Sheffield, in England.

"The child who is considered backward today may be the genius of tomorrow," Dr. Illingworth states. As an illustration of this he points to Albert Einstein, who was called "Mr. Dullard" by his teachers, and tossed out of one elementary school. He later flunked the entrance exam at the Polytechnic Academy in Zurich, Switzerland. Ludwig von Beethoven was described as "hopeless" in the area of musical composition by his teachers. Sir Isaac Newton—the man who discovered gravity—was at the bottom of most of his classes.

Winston Churchill, Dr. Illingworth points out, failed to get into prestigious Oxford or Cambridge Universities because he was weak in the classics. James Whistler, the painter, was expelled from West Point for failing chemistry.

Dr. Illingworth stresses that the failure of a child scholastically can lie in one of four places—the teacher, the parents, the child himself, or the method of assessing his knowledge, such as an examination.

It may give some comfort to parents of children who do poorly in some studies and solace to adults who still harbor feelings of inferiority over poor scholastic performance to remember that Franklin, Picasso, Adler and Jung were poor mathematicians; that Einstein, Poe, Shelley, Röntgen were expelled from school; that Edison was at the bottom of his class; that Gauguin was termed a dreamer by his teachers; that Watt was called "dull and inept" by a teacher, and that Yeats and Shaw were both poor spellers.

Many children who do badly in school are reacting to tension in the home. Some deficient performers are simply in unconscious rebellion against too much parental pressure; others have learning disabilities which need to be dealt with lovingly, patiently, and with understanding.

Isobel, my wife, once volunteered to teach a high school boy to read. He had been passed along from grade to grade although he could not read the simplest sentence. The school psychologist labelled him "unteachable." He came to our home two nights each week for some months. Isobel discovered the roots of his reading difficulty. His parents were rigid, authoritarian, religious fanatics. He had a poor relationship with his step-father, and a divorce had traumatized him as a small child. At first, most of the time was spent listening to the painful description of his home life and of the ridicule he received from other students because of his reading disability. He had come to believe that he was stupid, as they said he was. He was filled with self-hate and inferiority.

By the end of three months he was reading, slowly but acceptably. Within six months he was reading up to grade level. He did not lack intelligence, only understanding and loving acceptance, together with a new self-image.

Dr. James Watson, the scientist who shared the Nobel Prize for the discovery of the DNA code has only a high average I.Q. In discussing this, Dr. Watson said, "Some people thought I had a future anyway, because I asked questions and was curious. Persistent curiosity isn't shown by I.Q. tests." Nor, for that matter, is compassion, intuition, nor basic creativity. Psychologists now say that there may be 150 such factors which can be considered aspects of human intelligence, and I.Q. tests, often used to categorize children, measure very few of these traits.

Compassion for Children—a Recent Innovation

A study of historical sources reveals that loving, tender compassionate care of children is a fairly recent experience. Until the last century the beating of children was considered quite appropriate. Throughout history it was commonplace for children to be killed, abandoned, sexually abused and terrorized by adults. Virtually all treatises dealing with child-rearing, from antiquity through the middle of the eighteenth century, recommended the beating of children as an aid to discipline.

John Milton's wife complained that she could not stand the screams of his nephews as he beat them. Records indicate that Beethoven whipped his pupils with whatever was at hand. Even that loving paragon of motherhood, Susanna Wesley, said of her babies "when turned a year old and some before, they were taught to fear the rod and cry softly." Writer Rousseau reported that in his day young babies were often beaten to keep them quiet. Records tell of an early American mother who wrote of her battle with her four-month-old child, "I whipped him until he was actually black and blue, and until I could not whip him any more, and he never gave one single inch."

The eighteenth century pediatrician William Buchan is authority for the statement that almost half of the babies born died in infancy from improper care or neglect. Records show that of 21,000 children born in 1780 in Paris, 17,000 were sent into the country to be wet nursed, and 3,000 placed in nursery homes, while only 700 were nursed by their own mothers. It was common to take small children to the scenes of hangings to have them observe the rotting corpses hanging there as an example of what happened to disobedient children when they grow up. On occasion entire classes were taken out of school to witness public hangings. Parents were encouraged to whip their children afterwards so that they would remember what they had seen.

Polybus blamed the depopulation of Greece on the killing of unwanted children. The ratio of boys to girls ran four to one, since it was very rare for more than one girl in a family to be spared. Christians were viewed as peculiar because of their outspoken opposition to infanticide.

Ever so slowly, mankind makes progress. It is only by looking back into history that we gain the perspective which can prevent us from sinking into pessimism and despair.

A cartoon shows a father looking over his son's report card. The father is saying to the mother, "This report gives ample evidence that our son is not using any mind expanding drugs." An angry scene over a poor report card usually produces negative results. There is a growing body of evidence which validates the idea that two loving parents, with consistent discipline, produce children who tend to become mature, self-accepting, creative adults, with no need for alcohol, tranquilizers, or other anxiety reducers.

One psychologist, Dr. William R. Parker, suggests that the best combination of parents involves a mother who has strength behind her tenderness and a father whose strength is backed up by tenderness.

There Is No Blame

If you have children you may be asking, "What have I done to my children!" But, in common with the rest of the human race, you had parents who, however loving, made mistakes. If they were glaring ones, and if one or both parents were seriously marred, you are suffering in some degree from an inadequate early environment. This need not be fatal, for most of humanity has suffered from this malady. The important thing is to recognize the basic source of your personal defects. It is possible to trace a malfunction to its origin without condemnation. We need not accept personal blame for defects which originate in childhood. If we have added to these by our own mistakes, it may be that our difficulty in remedying the problem also originated in infancy or childhood. This is not an effort to excuse oneself at the expense of parents, but to trace the defect to its source. If our parents bear the major accountability for our malfunctioning personalities, we still bear an equal responsibility: to begin at this point to remedy the situation.

In later chapters we deal with means and methods for growing toward wholeness. For the moment we concern ourselves with the question of how we got the way we are and the manifold factors which contributed to our unease.

W. V. Caldwell writes, "Consider Leuner's patient . . . who spent twelve four-hour sessions hearing her parents scream and rail at each other. . . . By fusing these warring parental images they had become a part of herself. The parents were gone, no longer effective in her life, but the argument raged on in her soul. Without therapy she was doomed to bear the contempt of each for the other, in a life of internal bickering that would never end." [4]

In countless Primal Integration sessions dealing with infant and early childhood feelings, I have heard the pain, rage and horror of the child expressed in reaction to an unfeeling parent. There are a thousand variations, each constituting another validation of the idea that everything that happens to the child leaves its mark for good or evil, even though it is repressed and buried deep in the unconscious. The event is in the *past,* but the feelings are in the individual in the *present,* as fresh and vivid as the day of the occurrence. We have now learned, without drugs or hypnosis, to tap the unconscious and relieve it of its burden of terror and pain.

Sometimes the problem does not involve a defect on the part of the parent. A primal patient recently said, "It's dark—I'm frightened, terrified—it's awful. I can't go into it—I won't. I won't!" This was screamed out in terror as she brought herself back to the adult state. Then she said, "It was total darkness, and I was terrified, but I don't know of what. I had to shut it off; it was too horrifying."

I had observed similar reactions on other occasions, from other subjects. Almost inevitably this experience was the case of a small child awakening in a totally dark room, feeling helpless and afraid, wanting mother and not knowing how to get her to come, a sense of terror and hopelessness. Sometimes the fear seems to have originated in a dream. The important aspect of this type of therapy is that the reliving of the experience successfully discharges the anxiety encapsulating the event. Time does not diminish or erase ancient buried memories. They are alive and as damaging as when the original event first occurred. The vague, diffused anxiety from which so many people suffer, and its concomitant, generalized fatigue for which there is an apparent organic cause, often originates in these buried childhood terrors.

Children can be brutal and heartless in their relationship with other children. It is commonplace to see a small child biting another or hammering a sibling on the head with a toy. Older children often exhibit sadistic tendencies in their relationships. The assumption that this tendency is built-in, evidence of the total depravity of humankind, is wrong. This probably is not an inborn trait, but an unconscious way of "getting back" at someone after having suffered at the hands of an adult. A child who feels unloved and rejected, snapped at, screamed at, and made to feel humiliated, needs to express his unhappiness and anger. At whom? Certainly not at his parents. They are much too powerful. "Ah! I can pick on someone my own size, or preferably somewhat smaller. I can get revenge. I can do to them what my parents did to me. I can degrade them, humiliate them, scream at them, hit them just as I have been hit. Why not? Big people do it. I'll just pass it along."

Passing On Our Frustrations

Children who are abusive to pets are not little monsters by nature. A man told me that he had often heard the term *cat kicking,* but now he had seen it in action in his own home. Things had gone badly at work, and he had brought home a load of repressed anger which he couldn't appropriately express at the office. A minor argument erupted when he came home, and he shouted in a surly manner at his wife. A bit later he heard her yell at their five-year-old son. Later, head down and with a scowl, the boy went out into the yard with his dog. My friend said, "I happened to be watching when my son looked at his beloved dog. Suddenly he kicked the hapless dog and, simultaneously, screamed, 'Get away from me!' And all at once I was filled with remorse. I had brought this emotion home with me, passed it on to my wife, and she to our son, and he to his helpless little pet. I was terribly ashamed." If our children act like little monsters at times, it is because in some way, wittingly or otherwise, we have made them so.

It is not always the parent who stimulates the child's frustration. Sometimes it is other adults, such as teachers or relatives. From the age of five or six, a child spends more continuous hours with teachers than with parents. Just as there are parents who degrade children and cause them to despise themselves, so there are teachers who are impatient, demanding and degrading.

It is terribly demoralizing for a child to be molested sexually. An astounding number of women in Primal Integration sessions dredge up and relive such events, often buried in the unconscious.

My own observation, based upon scores of such cases, indicates that it is not the sexual pervert lurking in the bushes or in a parked car who is most likely to be the molester but, in this order, uncles, brothers, grandfathers, a trusted friend of the family, fathers, and finally, strangers. One woman, reliving such a traumatic event, came out of her session with the statement, "Why, it was my grandfather, and he was a pillar of the church, and taught Sunday school!"

The arousing of sexual feelings in a small child is particularly damaging because the tiny emotional structure of the child is unable to deal with such powerful emotions. The results can include frigidity, sexual promiscuity, neurosis and physical symptoms. It is not, incidentally, only little girls who are sexually mistreated; small boys are often molested sexually. Among the perpetrators of these crimes against children are youth leaders, family members, teachers, and friends of the family.

Learning to Despise Oneself

A child, made to feel inadequate and inferior, experiences a need to compensate in some way for the degradation suffered at the hands of others. One consequence mentioned by psychiatrist Karen Horney, "is the need to alleviate or balance self-contempt with the attention, regard, appreciation, admiration, or love of others. The pursuit of such attention is compulsive, because of the compelling need not to be at the mercy of self-contempt . . . and may amount to an all-consuming life goal. The result is total dependence on others for self-evaluation; it rises or falls with the attitude of others toward him." [5]

The neurotic comes to despise himself, as he felt himself to be rejected by others. He may dislike his face, his name, his body, his limitations, his mental faculties, or his performance as a human being. "The aggressive vindictive type, for instance, will despise in himself most deeply anything he conceives as 'weakness'." [6]

Sylvia, about thirty years old, felt contempt for herself without knowing precisely why. In early counseling sessions she told of her parents' divorce which had proven traumatic for her and made her feel rejected by her father, sexual molestation by a member of the family, and constant criticism by her father. She had no sense of self-worth whatever. She hated herself as she felt herself to have been degraded by others. This loss of self-respect and of a worthwhile self-image amounts to a loss of self, which Kierkegaard calls "sickness unto death" [7]—despair over the inability to feel a sense of worth; but this despair does not scream or cry out. Such people simply go on living a life of quiet, deadened desperation. They complain of physical symptoms, displaced from their emotional distress, or of some situational difficulty, but almost never do they say, "I don't know who I am. I have no identity. I am filled with despair and self-loathing."

Arnold was forty years old before he was able to break away from the influence of a domineering, sadistic mother and a passive father who conspired with his wife to keep him at home working in the family business. Under the pretext of coming to California on vacation, he left his home in the Midwest for what his parents imagined would be a temporary visit.

Arnold had been an active church member, but he was consumed by some nameless fear which made it impossible for him to speak in a group, to date, or to function normally in society. During extensive group experience, and a considerable number of Primal Integration sessions, he discovered the source of his difficulty. He became aware of an almost totally buried hostility toward his mother, a rage so deep that he had not dared to allow it into consciousness. Its power crippled and immobilized him. His was not an instant cure. He participated in a therapy group for over a year and experienced his primal hurts in scores of sessions before full relief came.

The result was the discharge of his self-hate, which at its core was hatred of the way he had been treated by his parents. By getting in touch with this legitimate anger (we have the right to be angry over being abused) he found himself, a new self-respect, a new career, and for the first time in his forty years, a genuine sense of fulfillment.

Until a person who has lost his selfhood can discharge the pent up hurt and anger, he "tends to feel what he *should* feel, wishes what he *should* wish, likes what he *should* like. In other words, the tyranny of the 'should' drives him frantically to be something different from what he is or could be. And in his imagination he *is* different—so different, indeed, that his real self fades. . . . " [8]

An important aspect of maturity and wholeness is the growing awareness that life is not simple, but very complex. Someone said in a group, "When I first discovered how complex life is, I was furious! Sometimes even now when I think about it, I get very angry."

The Need for Unconditional Love

This reaction is based on the fact that the child wants unconditional, uninterrupted love manifested in the form he desires, when he wants it, no matter how inconvenient or impossible this may be. Adults however must come to terms with the ambivalence of life, the many shades of truth and reality, the necessary compromises which must be made. Youth demands an absolute right, and an absolute wrong, and sees everything in black and white, no grays. Everything is pure good or pure evil. Maturing people, striving for wholeness, come to accept the fact that there are many shades of gray, and that there is not a vast deal of pure good, or pure evil, in the world.

Young men seek broad valid generalizations and, of course, there are a few of these. Integrated people recognize that there are a thousand exceptions and variables. "Every moment of experience forces man, grudgingly to sacrifice another chip from that monolithic granite of the mind which insists on the absolute, the exclusive, the pure and unqualified." [9]

It is my present conviction, subject to change if new evidence is forthcoming, that growth is the meaning of life. We are here to grow. Mistakes are not fatal; they are a part of life and development. Whatever is beyond the curtain of death, it certainly must involve further improvement. For he, who brought us sinless and stainless into an imperfect world and rejoiced over our birth, will surely not be content until we are whole and complete. The struggle to be more, love more, achieve more, and to become totally mature must go on into the infinite reaches of time until, without shame or pride, we shall deem ourselves ready to unite with him, the Pure Source of light and life.

3

Serenity, Stress and Anxiety

"Go very lightly on the vices such as
carrying on in society; the social ram-
ble ain't restful. Avoid running at all
times. Don't never look back over your
shoulder. Something might be gaining
on you."
—Attributed to Satchel Paige

Julian of Norwich, a monk who lived in England roughly a
thousand years ago, had a saying which came to be widely quoted
by his fellow monks. He used it in the face of bad news, disaster,
or undue concern. It was this: "All shall be well, and all shall be
well, and all manner of thing shall be well."

Picture this if you will: There is war in the land and food
shortages. Famine and panic are rampant in neighboring villages.
An epidemic breaks out. In the chapel, if we can give rein to our
imagination, Julian rises, a tall, serene figure in a patched brown
homespun robe. He says, "Peace, my brothers. All shall be well,
and all shall be well, and all manner of thing shall be well."

It is not only his words but his quiet poise which calms the over-
wrought monks. In modern parlance he was saying, "Relax, my
friends, relax! Times are hard and many are distraught; but in a
hundred years, or ten, or even a year from now, it won't really
matter. Be calm, serene. Do not let every rumor, or even disaster,
disturb your peace of mind. Take the long view. All shall be well,
and all shall be well, and all manner of thing shall be well. Calm
your spirits. We are dismissed. Go in peace."

Quiet Desperation

There are countless millions who are living lives of quiet desperation, rushed and hectic, driven by circumstances and inner disquiet.
The cartoon strip "B.C." once pictured two prehistoric characters
striding along rapidly. The first one asked, "Where are we going?"

The other replied, "Nowhere." The first character continued, "Then why are we going so fast?" This is a commentary on our modern stress-laden, harried, and hectic civilization. At a time when modes of travel have been speeded up fantastically, and housework and office routine simplified and made vastly more efficient, we are far more tense and anxious than our more leisurely horse and buggy forebearers with their woodburning cook stoves.

Something is wrong. Modern conveniences should have made us less rushed and more serene, but instead we are more anxiety-ridden than before. A British psychiatrist visiting the United States described Americans as "the most worried people in the world." It is a fact that we consume thirty-seven tons of aspirin a day, not to mention the millions of tranquilizers and sleeping pills.

Part of the problem lies in the fact that Americans are basically both idealistic and highly motivated. We are goal- and achievement-oriented. When we fail to reach our goals we become frustrated, tense and filled with anxiety. Extreme competitiveness marks the lives of most people, and this competitiveness diminishes the capacity for serenity.

Jim's father was a college president; his mother a widely known novelist. Though he did well in school, Jim lacked his father's tremendous drive and competitive spirit. After graduating from college Jim began teaching and did fairly well for two or three years, but became progressively more discontented. Finally he said to his father, "Dad, you and I don't have the same goals. I'm finding teaching kind of a bore. I don't want to spend ten or thirty years working toward some real or illusory goal of future happiness and contentment. I'd like some of that now. I'm going to drop out."

His father was horrified and began to protest. Jim stopped him. "Hold it, Dad. Hear me out. You and I know you aren't all that supremely happy. You've got ulcers, high blood pressure, and may or may not live to collect social security. You have all kinds of degrees and honors, but I don't value those things. I want some peace of mind; so I'm going to move to a small town I've picked out and become a cabinetmaker. I've always loved working with my hands. . . . "

"Jim, you can't. . . . " his father interrupted.

"Yes, I can. I can live my own life. I'm not dropping out of society, just out of the competitive race for prestige and recognition. It's fine for you if that's your thing; but I'm going to live a more leisurely life. I want to hunt and fish and have time to listen to my record collection. I want to enjoy the mountains. Dad, you know something? Just then when I said that, you looked positively wistful, as though you'd like to do some hunting and fishing too and take life a bit easier. . . ."

"Jim, someone has to run the schools and colleges, keep the economy going, administer the government. Everyone can't just flee to the mountains and putter at woodwork."

"Right. Everyone shouldn't do what I'm going to do, obviously. I respect those who want to push and organize and sweat; but I'm not wired-up that way. Are you willing to give me your blessing?" There was a long thoughtful silence. "Yes, son, of course; and part of me would like to join you, but I am too firmly committed to society's values, to my job; I'm too far along, too involved. But maybe I can find a way to cut loose from ulcer valley here and join you for some fishing occasionally."

When someone breaks out of the standard mold it usually creates considerable anxiety.

The Price of Status

A friend of mine, a talented minister serving as an associate on the staff of a thriving church, was once in a Yokefellow group which I happened to be leading. The group members each took a spiritual growth inventory [1] involving a psychological test with a feedback system of bi-weekly evaluation slips pointing up barriers to spiritual and emotional growth. My friend received a slip which I recalled some years later when he was permanently disabled by a serious heart attack. The slip read:

"You are so constituted emotionally and intellectually that you will function better and live longer in a secondary position rather than as a leader. Though you have many of the personal qualities of a leader, your emotional structure is such that leadership would provide undue stress. Accept the idea of being a first-class person in a secondary role—as vice-president rather than president, assistant rather than the director."

My friend, some of whose seminary classmates had achieved significant status, was not convinced. He accepted the pastorate of a large church where he did well, then became a denominational executive. He then suffered a disabling heart attack which ended his active life. His psychological profile had been accurate; but his drive for success and status had been so great that he disregarded it.

In the seeking of peace of mind and serenity, it must be recognized that there is no magic formula. One cannot violate one's personality and the laws of nature and gain serenity by repeating a pat phrase, or a Scripture verse daily.

However, there's another side to the coin. I knew a remarkable man, James L. Kraft, who founded the Kraft Cheese Company of Chicago many years ago. A devout and earnest Christian layman, Mr. Kraft served as the chairman of the board of his church for thirty years, spent one night a week calling for his church, was

Sunday School Superintendent for twenty-one years, and was active in denominational work, while he was president of the world's largest cheese company. He found ample time for recreation at Kraftwood, his Wisconsin lake retreat, and as a hobby he collected jade specimens and polished them in his hobby room at home.

Not everyone is constituted emotionally, intellectually and physically like J. L. Kraft. One must appraise his own capacities and temperament, and compete, not with others, but with his own previous best.

Women live six to eight years longer than men, but as more and more women move into positions of leadership in business, there is growing evidence that women, too, may begin to suffer from some of the tension-induced illnesses which afflict so many men.

Adults Who Obey Their Parents

It had been three months since Mary Ellen had experienced between thirty and forty hours of Primal Integration at our counseling center. She wrote me:

"As you know, I was a forty-two-year-old mother, wife and child. I am now a forty-two-year-old wife and mother, running my own life for the first time. Mother lived two miles away, and I was her little girl, thinking what she thought, doing what she wanted me to do, being a replica of her in every possible respect. It never occurred to me that I could or should be anything different until I ended up a year ago in a mental hospital with a psychotic break. I was there three weeks when a psychiatrist asked me how long I intended to let my mother dominate my life. I said, 'I don't know.' He couldn't seem to help me.

"In my primal sessions with you I finally got in touch with all of the repressed anger, frustration and rage at my loving, controlling, mind-sapping mother. I had no idea all that rage was down there! It had been there all my life, as I discovered. In those thirty or forty hours of primaling I got in touch with the real me for the first time. I have not rejected my mother, nor do I hate her. I love her as an adult friend, but I am no longer afraid to resist her unreasonable demands. She would come to my home three to five times a week unannounced, check on my activities in her cheerful, dominating way, correct my manners and attitudes, check on how I was raising my children, advise me on my marital relations, and in general take over my life. Now I have the courage to tell her firmly, gently, ruthlessly when I have other plans and cannot visit with her. I see her only once a week and refuse to talk to her by the hour on the phone. It took courage—I was scared—to tell her that I refused to be her little girl any longer. Her tears nearly wiped me out, but my adult self took over, and I refused to be manipulated by her martyrdom. Dad is quietly urging me on. It feels great to be a person in my own right at last. Almost all of the old anxiety and tension are gone. I never realized until those primal sessions that my life-long anxiety stemmed from holding down all of those negative feelings toward my controlling mother. Oh, incidentally, now that she doesn't spend all her time mothering me and my family, she has gotten into some community activities, and is really enjoying herself, to her surprise. . . ."

Imaginary Parental Control

Henry's case involved a different type of control. He said, "My father was a prosperous, right-wing Republican Methodist physician. I was never told directly that I was to be a carbon copy of my Dad; it was just an unquestioned assumption.

"After two frustrating years in medical school I realized I wasn't cut out to be a doctor. I quit school to take a job and do some thinking. Suddenly it dawned on me one day that I didn't *have* to be a doctor, a Republican, or a Methodist. It sounds stupid to say it, but for the first time I realized I was free to be a Lutheran, or a Catholic, and a dentist or a bill collector—whatever I desired to be. What a liberating idea! It blew my mind.

"Having made that big discovery I went back to school, only this time I took journalism. I wanted to be a writer. I loved it. Eventually I became an agnostic and an independent voter registered as a Democrat. Gradually I abandoned the rebellious agnostic stance and, at forty, ended up a Presbyterian, a right-wing Democrat, and a writer, happy in my profession. It feels good to be me, instead of a carbon copy of my Dad, whom I love more than ever. Dad heartily approved of my switch to writing and said, 'Son, I never cared whether you were a doctor, lawyer or bricklayer so long as you were happy.' Following in his footsteps had been my own idea all along, not his, only I didn't know it."

Demands, Expectations and Preferences

It usually makes us frustrated or unhappy when our demands or expectations are not met by others. A puzzled and frustrated husband said to me in a counseling session, "I had always assumed that people fell in love, got married, and met each other's needs. My wife didn't meet my expectations, so I made some demands. To my surprise she said I wasn't meeting her needs either. We reached an angry impasse. Where do we go from here? How do we resolve the conflict? She's so damned unreasonable!"

I said, "My friend, both you and your wife have approached

marriage with unrealistic expectations and demands. This is not
an uncommon experience. Most couples have similar conflicts. The
answer, easy to state but somewhat more difficult to accomplish,
is to give up demands and expectations, and settle for *preferences*.
When we make demands on other people we arouse anger, or at
least resentment. It makes the other person feel controlled. We
humans all tend to resent being dominated."

"But what if she doesn't meet either my expectations or my
preferences? What then?"

"You and your wife will both have to agree to give up demands
and expectations, and settle for preferences, *simultaneously*. It is
more a manner, a tone of voice and facial expression than of words.
It must originate in an inner willingness to stop trying to force or
control each other. Back off. Stop trying to get all of your needs
met by your wife. No one person can meet all of your needs. Five
wives probably couldn't meet all of them. Start finding out what
her needs are. List them; write them down and examine them every
day. Ask her what needs she has which you aren't meeting and do
your best to meet as many of those as you can. You'll find that when
you do, she will respond with more love and affection, and she will
begin trying to meet *your* needs. Let her know your needs gently
and lovingly, without criticism. All criticism is perceived as an
attack. Remember, express them as preferences, rather than as demands. If she cannot meet all of them at once, give her time. You'll
need time, too, to learn how to meet her needs. Abandon criticism,
demands, and retaliation. Take Jesus literally: 'Give, and it will be
given to you.' " [2]

I recall teachers whose very manner made me bristle. Learning
with them was a grim business, though every enlightened educator
knows—or at least has been taught—that pupils learn best in a
happy atmosphere. Then there were other teachers under whom it
was a joy to study. They made no demands, only mildly expressed
expectations or preferences, but because I felt their warmth and
caring, I was far more motivated to learn than with the grim
purveyors of knowledge.

The same thing holds true in husband and wife relationships:
demands or stridently expressed expectations usually produce either
anger or at least resentment. My wife has just dismantled the Christmas tree, stored the ornaments, and written an enormous batch of
thank-you notes, including some which I should have written; but
she knew I was busy and didn't bother me. During a pause in my
typing I asked her if she were finished. She said, "Yes, I got the
Christmas tree out in the yard to be hauled away but the metal
stand is still attached. Could you do that sometime?" Feeling

slightly guilty over not having helped dismantle the tree, I said, "Of course. Right away." Had she come on with a martyred complaint about how hard she had worked, together with a strong, "And you've got to finish it up and remove the tree stand," I might have reacted a little differently. I would have done it, of course, but with a vague anxiety gnawing at me inside somewhere; because a wife who sounds like a mother nagging a lazy teenager can create a certain amount of resentment.

New Attitudes Can Be Acquired

It is not easy to achieve new attitudes. It takes time. A teacher at an adult center told of having asked her class to write and turn in their goals for the new year in terms of self-improvement. She promised to post them on the bulletin board. Passing the board one day, she noticed a young woman searching for her resolutions. Suddenly she said loudly to two others standing by, with angry vehemence, "My resolution isn't posted, and it was one of the first ones in!" The teacher rushed back to her desk and found the missing resolution under some other papers. It read, "I resolve not to let little things upset me." It is far easier to make a resolution than to establish a whole new set of reactions.

This takes time, but can pay big dividends. Write this down and put it where you can look at it daily:

> Serenity is the art of learning
> to view life, myself, and others
> with amused, friendly tolerance

Don't be disappointed if you don't achieve that goal in a day, or even in six months. Any new habit takes time and constant repetition to make it a permanent part of one's personality. Few young people have serenity or peace of mind to any significant degree, because it requires time and patience to achieve this.

I was the youngest member of my seminary graduating class, very green and inexperienced. To my enormous surprise I was called to a reasonably large city church. I dared not permit myself to know how frightened I was, but the amount of fear which reached my conscious mind was large enough to keep me in a constant state of tension and anxiety.

Terror would have been a better word. This insidious, demoralizing terror hit me every Sunday morning as I began to dress. I had expected to start out in some less threatening, small-town church, but suddenly I was thrust into a situation beyond both expectation and capacity. By the time breakfast was over my stomach was in a frightful turmoil. My mouth was dry. I managed to present an apparent outward calm, but inwardly I was a quaking mass of insecurity and anxiety. After a month or so of this I asked myself the question, "What would happen if I were to fail completely this morning and make an absolute fool of myself?" That, I thought, would be very embarrassing; "I wouldn't like it. But ten years from now, or even a year from today, it won't matter," I added to myself.

Every Sunday morning when the stomach-tightening tension started I used the same approach, talking to my fears. "So what if I make a fool of myself? Big deal. It isn't the end of the world." Finally I gave myself permission to fail completely. I accepted the idea of failure, finally, with reasonable complacency. In the back of my mind I knew that the less I cared the more relaxed I would be, and thus more effective. The problem was, I cared too much; but when I talked myself into not caring—or caring less—the anxiety subsided. Within a month or less the inner panic had become a more or less normal apprehension, and I functioned much better.

Serenity and Lowered Expectations

There is no quick, easy way to achieve serenity, for it involves many things: the lowering of our expectations and demands, the conquering of excessive tension and anxiety, and the cultivation of a trust in God, life, and people. It can take years, or half a lifetime, to achieve a measure of serenity. Some, who are reared in a less anxiety-producing environment, achieve serenity with much less effort. Others, who did not receive adequate love in childhood, or whose lives have been tension-filled and frustrating, find it much more difficult.

Janet had been married for twenty-six years and separated for seven of those years. Her husband, a heavy drinker, lived with his mistress, but insisted on seeing his wife several times a week. He virtually controlled her life. She could not endure living with him because of his drunken rages, but she could not bring herself to cut loose from him entirely. He resisted the idea of divorce for financial reasons.

In some Primal Integration sessions where Janet got in touch with her buried feelings toward her mother, she came to see that she had the same fearful, dependent, masochistic relationship with her husband as she had with her mother. One day she exclaimed after a session, "Good heavens! I married my mother and just continued the process of being beaten down and controlled. He and my mother treated me the same way, and I let them get away with it! I couldn't defend myself against Mother, and haven't against George, but that's going to change."

"What do you intend doing?" I asked.

"I'm going to get a divorce! It's long overdue. I've been afraid to do it, but now I know I can face the future without letting him control my life."

When she broke the news to him, she told me later, he went into one of his towering rages. "But," she said, "instead of dissolving into tears as I usually do, I stood my ground, and when his tantrum resembled the antics of a child more than the attitude of an adult, I found myself laughing at him. What a switch! It feels great to be in control of my own life and emotions after all these years."

We cannot become serene, happy individuals until we are in control of our own lives. If we are "other-directed"—fearfully trying to meet the unrealistic expectations of others—we become passive puppets rather than free persons.

The "Hurry Sickness"

Blue Cross, in one of their bulletins, wrote, "Your personality more than obesity, high blood pressure, elevated cholesterol, even cigarette smoking could make you a prime candidate for a heart attack. The most likely coronary victim under age sixty is hurried, impatient, and constantly under stress from an urgent, pressing feeling that he hasn't enough time. Body movements are brisk, fists frequently clenched. He speaks in explosive hurried speech, and his body always seems tense."

To cure "hurry sickness" they advise the following:

Realize that relaxation is not a luxury but a necessity.
Eliminate unnecessary events and activities.
Get up fifteen minutes earlier to have more time to dress and talk to the family.
Slow down your pace of eating and drinking.
Take time alone to read, dream, and analyze your life.

Stress, usually originating in inner tension and conflict, is the great enemy of serenity and wholeness. The overly-ambitious, tense individual, scarcely aware of his inner tension, is usually driven by nameless forces. In most instances such a person will not slow down until there is a crisis: a heart attack or some other serious warning. Like the alcoholic who will not attend Alcoholics Anonymous or take other steps toward a cure until there is a crisis in his life ("hitting bottom," AA calls it) so a workaholic will usually not slow down and reorder his life until there is a warning serious enough to stop him in his tracks.

Many a sermon is preached offering the infinite "peace that passes understanding" once you have accepted Christ and joined the

church. When your sins are forgiven and you enter a new relationship with Christ all will be well. Stress and anxiety will disappear
as if by magic; false values give way to supreme values, and all life
takes on new meaning. Relationships all become imbued with the
spirit of Christian love, and a kind of pink euphoria settles over
everything.

And it does seem to work that way for a few people: why not for
everyone? To be perfectly honest and realistic, we must admit that
for uncounted millions of Christians life is not lived in a state of
euphoric bliss. Making a profession of faith is not guaranteed to
give you peace of mind and serenity.

A fine Christian businessman said, "I have believed all the fundamentals of the faith most of my life, and I am a faithful church
member, but it has not cured my ulcers, improved my marriage,
nor given me the inner peace I have heard promised so often.
Where have I gone wrong?"

To begin with, many a sermon promises dividends and blessings
not authorized in the Bible. The Apostle Paul suffered innumerable
hardships despite intense loyalty to Christ. Jesus died on a cross,
some of the Twelve were martyred, others driven into exile. Jesus
said, "In the world you have tribulation; but be of good cheer,
I have overcome the world." [3]

Christians Can Have Problems

At the risk of seeming to deprecate the Christian experience, I
would point out that one may be living a dedicated Christian life
and still experience such things as an impaired marriage, physical
illness, bankruptcy, death of a loved one, the loss of friends, and
other major or minor disasters. I have known splendid Christians
who tithed and later went bankrupt; devoted Christian workers
who had mental breakdowns; ministers who were subject to fits of
deepest depression, Sunday school teachers whose children committed suicide. Being a Christian is no guarantee of success in
business, nor does it guarantee freedom from sickness, sorrow, or
failure. I deplore the implication that the Christian is going to live
such a "victorious life" that he will be untroubled by disease, disaster or despair. What Christ does offer us is strength to overcome,
to win out in the end, to withstand whatever happens to us. Peace
of mind does not come from the absence of problems and difficulties, but from the ability to cope with them.

Something in us secretly longs for the serenity of an island paradise or, more realistically, a few acres and a home in a rustic setting,
away from the rush, smog and conflict of the city. These are legitimate longings, originating partly in a desire to escape life's tensions,

but partly rooted, no doubt, in a racial memory of a long-forgotten Garden of Eden; yet, even there, temptation and sin entered and the erring pair were driven from their sylvan paradise to earn their living, even as we, by the sweat of their brow. There was conflict and stress even in the Garden.

Stress Is a Part of Life

Dr. Hans Selye, who has been studying stress for nearly forty years, and whose discoveries in the field are generally accepted by medical men, states that "Stress is not merely 'nervous tension . . .' Stress is not something to be avoided. In common parlance, when we say someone is under stress, we actually mean under excessive stress or distress—just as the statement 'he is running a temperature' refers to an abnormally high temperature.

"Stress," Dr. Selye says, "is the non-specific response of the body to any demands made on it. . . . It is immaterial whether the agent or situation we face is pleasant or unpleasant; all that counts is the intensity of the demand for readjustment or adaptation. The mother who is suddenly told that her only son died in battle suffers a terrible mental shock; if years later it turns out that the news was false and the son unexpectedly walks into her room alive and well, she experiences extreme joy. Her sorrow and joy are opposites, yet their effects as stressors may be the same.

"It is difficult to see how such different things such as cold, heat, drugs, hormones, sorrow and joy can provide an identical biochemical reaction in the body. Nevertheless, it can now be shown by highly objective, biochemical determination that certain reactions are . . . common to all stress." [4]

Stress, in moderate amounts, Dr. Selye points out, is an essential ingredient of life. We might avoid stress by total inactivity, but who, he asks, could enjoy life with no hits, no runs, no errors.

The best way to avoid stress in harmful amounts is to select an environment where you feel reasonably comfortable. The environment may consist of husband, wife, boss, friends, job. One's vocation should ideally provide a normal amount of tension and stress, but not an undue amount. It is the need to adapt and readapt constantly to frustrating, stress-producing situations that robs life of its serenity and happiness.

We usually think of excessive stress and tension as being by-products of modern civilization, but Dr. J. David Kinzie, professor of psychiatry at the University of Hawaii, and Dr. J. Malcolm Bolton, senior medical officer and medical director at Gompak Hospital in West Malaysia, have found acute schizophrenia existing in even the remote interior jungle areas where primitive people still hunt with blow pipes and poison darts. These people, living under idyllic conditions, are trained never to harm another human being. Yet, even among such peaceful, primitive people living in the wild, there is evidence of emotional distress originating in inner conflict.

In discussing aging in relation to tension and stress, Dr. Selye states that "aging results from the sum of all the stresses to which the body has been exposed during a lifetime. Each period of stress—especially if it derives from frustration and unsuccessful struggles—leaves some irreversible chemical scars, which accumulate to constitute the signs of tissue aging." [5]

But any form of *successful* activity, regardless of how intense, leaves one with fewer scars. Intense efforts resulting in a successful outcome, leave one with a feeling of exhilaration. It is frustration and failure, more than work, which step up the aging process.

Aging Gracefully and Dynamically

One may point to Winston Churchill, Henry Ford, Charles de Gaulle, Titian, Michaelangelo, Rubenstein, Pablo Cassals, Queen Victoria and a host of others who were alive, vigorous and active into their eighties and nineties.

Supreme Court Justice Holmes, who was still going to work daily in his nineties, was taking a walk one day with a friend about the same age when a very attractive woman in her mid-fifties paused to speak to them and then walked on. Holmes looked at his aged friend and sighed, "Oh, to be eighty again!"

These people and many more like them lived active, busy lives, but with a seeming leisureliness. It is as if they were flowing with life, rather than pushing, straining and struggling.

It would not be accurate or truthful to imply that everyone can live a stress-free, leisurely, successful life into the late eighties or nineties, free of undue anxiety or tension. There is such a thing as heredity, a genetic heritage, which can give one a powerful boost in the right direction. There is also the matter of environment. There are people who have been blessed or crippled by their early environment. Yet, along with forces which can help or hinder growth and fulfillment, there is the matter of free will. I cannot become *anything*, but I can become *something*. At the very least I can become more of a whole person through careful introspection, reckoning my assets and acknowledging my weaknesses. I can be more, achieve more, love more, grow more; for emotional and spiritual growth is the meaning of life. God lures us on toward this growth as a patient, loving father coaxes a faltering child just learning to walk. God does not condemn us when we fall, but how he rejoices when we rise and try again!

4

Religion and Wholeness

> "He was, and is yet most likely, the most wearisome, self-righteous Pharisee who ever ransacked the Bible to rake the promises to himself and fling the curses to his neighbors."
> —Emily Bronte, of Joseph, the old manservant.

I have always thought of it as the Battle of the Hymnbooks. Our family had moved to a tiny Texas town, with no paved streets or sidewalks, a two-room school and a one-room frame church. It was in this little church that I absorbed some of my earliest religious concepts.

Three of us small boys were paid fifteen cents each to arrive at church an hour early and clean it up. We were to sweep, dust, and rearrange the hymnbooks. It was no bargain for the church, since we were rather poor custodians, though no one complained. Had they done so, it might have opened them up to the possibility of having to do the work themselves, of being forced to raise our minuscule wages, or of finding some other boys to replace us, an incredibly difficult recruitment task, since no other boys in their right minds would have considered such shameful wages.

We were usually moderately earnest, in a relaxed way, about our sweeping and dusting, but one fine Sunday morning, having completed our work a bit early, we grew playful. One of the boys ("a lewd fellow of the baser sort," though it is conceivable that I could have been the one) threw a hymnbook at someone. Suddenly there erupted what will go down in history as the greatest hymnbook fight ever to take place in a small Texas town. The air was filled with books, loose pages flying every which way. Covers came off, and the ancient hymnals disintegrated. It was an exciting battle.

45

Adrenaline flowed and stirred the pulses. Joyous cries of "Gotcha!" rang out. Oh, it was great fun.

It was, that is, until a strident voice rang out from the doorway. "Well, I never!" It was dear old Mrs. Whipple. Sudden sanity prevailed, and frantically we began the hopeless task of gathering up backless hymnals, fitting loose pages approximately into their proper places. As I glanced about I saw that it was a disaster area, but before much could be done to remedy the situation my father's stern face appeared. The memory of what happened thereafter has been mercifully blotted from my memory, for it was too dreadful to have been retained in my conscious mind.

Yet, I have some pleasant memories associated with that little church, whose members seemed to me even then to be a fascinating mixture of saint and sinner, spiritual giant and pious fraud.

A Frowning, Judgmental God

It was there that I learned that God could see through brick walls, and that he was out to get me. When I thought of him he seemed to be wearing a perpetual frown, like my father and, as my father, he was never relaxed. He wanted me to be in constant motion. God took a dim view of my wretchedly sinful nature, and no matter how hard I tried I could never seem to please either God or my father. They seemed to merge in some indefinable way.

And, blackest of all black thoughts, I had occasional doubts, and obsessive thoughts which ran around repetitiously in my mind— evil thoughts, shameful ideas, awful temptations. It was not easy being a Christian, I discovered.

The church came to mind vividly when I read this passage from a book written by the president of a conservative theological seminary:

> The gospel, we boldly insist, is not *an* answer, one among many; it is *the* answer.
> But before we become too serenely complacent that we possess the panacea secular psychiatrists are still seeking to find and formulate, we had better candidly admit that Christianity sometimes seems to be an impotent failure in solving the problems that plague people.
> A few years ago, for instance, I sat in a church sharing as a visitor in its monthly observance of the Lord's supper. Holding in my hand the cup which symbolizes the reconciling sacrifice of Jesus Christ, I had difficulty focusing attention on Calvary. . . . I happened to know rather intimately the history of that struggling fellowship. So, as I sat there holding in my hand the symbol of heaven's healing for earth's sinful sickness, I thought of the

pastor who in bitterness and brokenness had left that church. I thought of the psychic climate which prevailed within its small congregation—the divisiveness, the contentiousness, the suspiciousness, the defensiveness, the pettiness, the smugness, the exclusiveness, the phoniness, the loneliness, and the unhappiness.

I realized that an unkind outsider might have stigmatized that group as a Christian ghetto—a little clique of pious bigots, as a cynic once sneered. . . . By the most charitable of criteria that fellowship was really sick. Healing and reconciliation, freedom and abundant living were not noticeably its earmarks.[1]

The author strikes me as an honest and candid observer of the human scene. In a subsequent passage he describes the anguish of a young woman serving as a missionary overseas. She had spoken of some friends who had recently become Christians, and then, "shaken by emotion, she exclaimed that she was trying to keep them from attending her own church. She was afraid that among the unsaintly saints she had learned to tolerate, saints who were evidently narrow and nasty, her friends would become disillusioned with Christianity. Heatedly she exclaimed, 'I don't want them spiritually ruined by my church! . . .' Having inhabited the ecclesiastical world for a long time, I could sympathize with her fears. Many biblically oriented churches, I was and am keenly aware, are seriously sick, even as I realize that many Christians are by no means shining examples of healthy-mindedness." [2]

Man Is Incurably Religious

As far back as the records go, man has been incurably religious. I have visited Stonehenge, the Egyptian pyramids, Machu Piccu, Knossis, the Temple of Luxor, Chichen Itza, and Teotihuacan; I have studied the ruins in Puebla in Mexico, Balbek, Tikal, Corinth, Ephesus, the temples of ancient Greece, Babylon, the Acropolis, Petra and Jerash. I searched in Bali, Iraq, Iran, and Kathmandu, Nepal. All but Machu Piccu dealt with religion and ultimate reality in some way. Most had religious centers or were centers or worship. Yes, man has always been religious, and always will be.

Former Premier Khrushchev once said, "Thank God we Russians are not hanging on to old religious fables!" Though at an intellectual level he was an atheist, his emotional nature still clung to the religious concepts of his childhood. His slip of the tongue when he said, "Thank God, . . ." betrayed vestigial remains of a faith older than his atheism. Yes, man is incurably religious, but there are a thousand variations on the religious theme.

The religiously immature try to make God a kind of cosmic errand-boy who, as long as they are in favor with him by staying moderately religious, will do their bidding, protect them from harm, and see to it that they become prosperous. Though we recognize intellectually that some people will perish in plane crashes and others die a lingering death of cancer, it will not happen to us, for we have the magic of believing. When this fails to work we feel let down, disillusioned, and angry. One way to hit back at this illusory God is to stop believing in him. What's the use of believing in a God who doesn't protect and prosper you?

Of course, what we stop believing in—for the moment at least—is a god of our own invention, who bears no relation to the God and father of Jesus Christ. For Jesus asked no special favors of his Father, who even allowed him to go to the cross.

And there on the cross Jesus could cry out in agony, "My God, why . . . ?" True, this is a quotation from the Psalm 22, but Jesus chose those words to express what was in his heart. Questioning, doubting, uncertainty are all part of life, and one need not imagine he is losing his faith if he experiences doubts.

The Enemy Is Us

There are blatant and obvious weaknesses evident in the institutional church, but they are the corporate faults of humankind. As Pogo put it, "We have met the enemy and he is us." I have only to look within to find, if I look diligently, that I have traces of the very defects I deplore in the meanest, most unforgiving, and judgmental church. The only thing which could prevent my admitting it would be a monumental pride, a sin as great as those I criticize in others.

Even so, I deplore the kind of sermons which are judgmental, nit-picking, condemnatory, legalistic. I find it difficult not to say to such preachers, "My friend, psychologically we know what troubles you. You are able to keep your own guilty feelings suppressed only by angry denunciation of the sins you see in others. The vehemence of your condemnation links you, not so much with the prophets, as with the Pharisees."

Carl Michalson has written, "Christianity is not a litigation of the human race; it is a vindication, a therapy, a healing. . . . Jesus is not the accuser; Satan is. The early fathers of the church, like Polycarp, were inclined to condemn the theologically irregular, but they were almost as gentle as Jesus with the morally irregular. The total witness of the Christian community is alien to condemnation, for its mission and message is reconciliation. . . . The guilt of man is not the truth; it is the lie. The truth is that God wills to have fellowship with sinners. . . . He takes the consequence of their sin upon himself." [3]

There is a natural tendency to suppose that people were more religious in the past. Many secular writers, some of whom seem not to have spent more than a weekend west of the Hudson, continue to write of the "great decline in religious belief." They have not done their homework.

Church membership in the 1770s was only six to eight percent of the population according to historians. The Great Awakening of the middle third of the century was followed by the Big Sleep, and the Revolutionary era was a period of decline for American Christianity, according to Yale's religious historian Sydney Ahlstrom. He points out that the churches reached the lowest ebb of vitality during the two decades after the end of hostilities than at any time in the nation's history.

In the midst of the War for Independence, the Continental Congress implored the nation to beseech God that "vice, profaneness, extortion, and every evil may be done away . . . that we may be a reformed and happy people." We have come to think of our ancestors as moral and ethical people, so it comes as a shock to learn that Washington had to chase a horde of Philadelphia prostitutes from Valley Forge, and that five hundred "ladies of pleasure" lived in an area called Holy Ground because it was owned by Trinity Church in New York.

In Groton, Massachusetts, one-third of the two hundred people who joined the church between 1761 and 1775 confessed to fornication. A small Episcopal church in Maryland chastised thirteen fornicators or adulterers in a single month. "The fact that there were confessions and corrections shows that simple permissiveness did not prevail, but neither did simple virtue." [4]

Martin Marty points out that "gambling was universal, and fighting was taken in stride. Preachers fretted about English-inspired 'foppery, luxury and recreation . . .' A prohibitionist in colonial America would have been considered a lunatic. The alcoholic eye-opener was a morning ritual for some upper-class women. . . . On the Carolina frontier, Episcopalian Charles Woodmason grumbled that 'both Presbyterians and Episcopalians very charitably agree on Getting Drunk.' " [5]

Religion and Legalism

Wholeness cannot be equated with religiosity. Marjorie's favorite phrase was, "I'm happy in the Lord." She was widely praised for her enthusiasm, her religious dedication, and her vast knowledge of the Scriptures. Her spirituality was very legalistic and fundamentalist. Her one child, a daughter, got an early dose of this almost from infancy. When the daughter was nine or ten she proceeded to rebel violently, and her rebellion continued through high school. Although she had been the recipient of love from both parents, the fact that her mother was so excessively "religious" seemed to be the root of her rebellion. Soon after graduating from high school she married a very immature young man from whom she was speedily divorced; the second husband and she became drug addicts, and later both committed suicide.

Marjorie's religion appeared to be excessively moralistic and rigid. She would not attend a movie, not even a Walt Disney film, for fear her influence might affect someone adversely, but she was the first person in her church to purchase a TV set when they became available. Can a person be "too religious"? Apparently so. Too much of anything is too much.

One factor which prevents my feeling too judgmental about such instances of religious excessiveness, is the memory of a time in my youth when I was somewhat legalistic in my own religious views. I can recall my great distress at hearing a minister state that the Apostle Paul was wrong in his belief that Christ's second coming would occur in the immediate future. Without examining the evidence I sallied forth, booted and spurred, and rode off in all directions, determined to defend the idea that every statement in the Bible was to be taken literally. Today when I find someone attempting to apply Paul's first-century dress codes and behavior patterns to twentieth-century Christians, I wince with the remembrance of my own youthful errors in matters no less absurd.

America is essentially a religious nation, despite all evidences to the contrary. Martin Marty has pointed out that "a hundred million Americans see God as 'the giver of all goodness' through his gift of grace in Jesus Christ." Newspaper headlines, radio and TV news broadcasts gather up a thousand evidences of moral depravity and spill it out before us, while the ten thousand acts of moral grandeur and a million acts of compassion and love go unrecorded.

Commenting on the general tone of religion in the United States, even if it is sometimes distorted, John Burton said, "America is a place where Jewish merchants sell Zen love beads to agnostics for Christmas."

There are a thousand distortions of Christianity, as of any important truth. Clarence Day said of his father, that "he was always trying to bring this or that to pass, only to find that there were obstacles in the way. . . . He didn't actually accuse God of gross inefficiency, but when he prayed his tone was loud and angry, like that of a dissatisfied guest in a carelessly managed hotel." A thousand spiritual or moral failures or ridiculous distortions do not constitute a denial of God's truth.

The Church—Our Last, Best Hope

In the course of the years I have conducted retreats and weekend seminars in a large number of churches, representing a dozen or more denominations. Although they were of all sizes and kinds, representing many shades of theological belief, from extreme conservative to liberal, they all had so much in common that I could seldom remember the denomination afterward. My overall impression of those churches is that they were not exclusive clubs for the spiritually elite, but a gathering place for all who were hurting and wanted relief and all who were compassionate and wanted to help. The Church is the most effective institution on earth for general spiritual growth. A vast deal of therapy takes place on Sunday mornings all across the land.

Not all of the spiritual giants are enrolled as church members. Albert Einstein once said in an address, that "the most beautiful and most profound emotion we can experience is the sensation of the mystical. It is the dower of all true science. He to whom this emotion is a stranger, who can no longer wonder and stand rapt in awe, is as good as dead. To know that what is impenetrable to us really exists, manifesting itself as the highest wisdom and the most radiant beauty which our dull faculties can comprehend only in their most primitive forms—this knowledge, this feeling is at the center of true religiousness."

This is an anxiety-producing world, and failure to find a satisfying religious faith opens the door to excessive amounts of anxiety for millions of people. Faith in the eternal goodness of God, as manifested in Christ, helps finite man to accept his humanity, as well as his divinity. Man is all too aware of his guilt, the certainty of his ultimate death, and the uncertainty of the future. He needs a fixed point to which he can cling, a faith so deep that he can say, as someone has expressed it, "I would still believe, though I woke in hell." Belief in the ultimate triumph of good, when "the kingdom of this world . . . belongs to our Lord, and to his Christ; and he shall reign forever and ever" [6] is the ultimate answer to the pervasive anxiety which afflicts so much of humankind.

God's Secrets

Mankind has long sought a broad spectrum remedy for human ills of the flesh, and for society at large. As a small boy I heard many debates concerning women's suffrage. The anti forces were certain that women going to the polls would destroy the home; whereas the pro element insisted with equal vehemence that once women were given the vote it would be the end of war, for "no mother would ever vote to send her son to war." Society would feel the tender touch of womankind's compassionate hand, and crime would cease, evil would be banished and, we were assured, the Kingdom of Heaven would come.

Equally futile have been many other naïve hopes and dreams.

The first issue of *Radio Broadcast,* launched early in 1922, predicted that radio broadcasting would "elicit a new national loyalty and produce a more contented citizenry. . . . The government will be a living thing to its citizens instead of an abstract and unseen force. Elected representatives will not be able to evade their responsibility to those constituents who put them in office. The People's University of the Air will have a greater student body than all the rest of our universities together." That same year, former Secretary of the Navy, Josephus Daniels, joined in the predictions with the pronouncement that "nobody now fears that a Japanese fleet could deal an unexpected blow on our Pacific possessions. . . . Radio makes that impossible." Magazine articles of the day featured such titles as "How Radio Is Remaking the World," "Radio, the Modern Peace Dove," and "Ether Waves Versus Crime Waves." So much for the belief that new inventions or laws will alter human nature, bring world peace, and abolish sin, suffering and sorrow. We are forced to acknowledge the idea that if the world is to be saved from the insanity of war, crime, poverty and assorted human ills, it will come about because of the message proclaimed by Jesus. If we live it and proclaim it the world will feel its impact.

While having a leisurely trip through various parts of Europe which we had only skimmed before, Isobel and I paused in Geneva to visit Dr. Paul Tournier, who had once visited in our home, and whose books have blessed and inspired so many people. After lunch at our hotel he drove us to his home for an extended visit, during which I asked about his newest book, then in preparation. It dealt with aggression which, as he pointed out, can be used for good or evil. He spoke of the way in which God touches some people and enables them to use this aggression in creative ways. I asked, "How do you account for the fact that God touched you, and not Adolph Hitler?" He smiled and replied, "Ah! That is God's secret!"

Intellectually we may acknowledge that we can never have all the answers, but at a feeling level we reject the idea of the unknown and of mysteries; we want to have final answers, for if there are no unanswered questions we will be less anxiety-ridden. A growing faith in the infinite God, most of whose purposes and methods are hidden, can relieve our anxiety.

Dr. Eli Chesen points out that a great many people experience a vague and pervasive depression because of their philosophy or early religious training. He sees this as prevalent among people who were reared in a judgmental and dogmatic religious environment, among college students, college professors and intellectually oriented people in general.

It is the result, he believes, of their belief or feeling that ours is a randomly organized and purposeless universe in which man resides accidentally. "He, therefore, lives without purpose and is doomed to an existence which is antagonistic to nature. Man ultimately dies and nature goes on without him as if he never existed." [7]

Dr. Chesen says that "a disproportionate number of atheists I have known seem to be preoccupied with the thought that they are merely specks of dust, parasites on a larger speck of dust, and so on. They arrive at their conclusions through . . . logic, which is intellectually fulfilling, but spiritually empty." He also points out that after seeing a fair number of people with terminal illnesses, "though few are happy at the thought of death, the person without a religious faith is often the most angry and uncomfortable. Religious persons seem more accepting and tolerant of their final days. They approach death not as an end, but as transition."

The Unpredictability of God

One of the surprising things about God is his unpredictability. Jane was quite depressed and hopeless when she came to our counseling center [8] for several weeks of Primal Integration. In one session Jane, who had no religious background or belief whatever, began to breathe heavily as though under some powerful emotional experience. This went on for over half an hour. Finally, when she could speak, she said, ecstatically, "He touchced me! It was Christ, and he came toward me, and stretched out his arms to me. He smiled, and he forgave me. . . ." She still had her eyes closed, and her face was lit up with a glorious radiance. "It was beautiful. It happened to me, Jane! He came to me, a waitress, to me, Jane! He's beautiful . . . wonderful!" She lay there for some time absorbing and enjoying the thrilling experience. Hours later she was still ecstatic.

I became aware of a sudden irrational and unworthy thought: Why doesn't that happen to me? She doesn't even have a religious background or Christian beliefs. Then that thought was instantly banished by the picture of Jesus followed by a rabble who had no particular religious convictions, and I thought of the woman who washed his feet with her tears, the blind beggars, and the rabble whom the Pharisees called sinners. His followers were not, by ordinary standards, "the best people." Then I listened again to Jane, and as I rejoiced with her I began to have a religious experience of my own, just by seeing the rapture on her face. Yes, God is very unpredictable. He cannot be put in a box or contained in a set of religious beliefs. The truth is that we don't really know a vast deal about God, except that he is like Jesus, and that is enough to challenge us for the rest of our lives.

Wholeness or "Goodness"?

I deplore the equating of Christianity with "being good." There are great ethical and moral implications in the gospel of Jesus, but it's interesting to note that Jesus never urged anyone to be "good." He did not even use such terms as *good* or *bad*, but he did ask, "Do you want to be made whole?" Morality and decency and ethical behavior should ideally spring from wholeness, rather than be the product of a rigid code of behavior. I would urge you to stop trying to be "good," and try to obey the supreme law which involves loving God and your fellow man as yourself. If you do this your conduct will take care of itself. The religious zealot would require you to believe his set of doctrines and obey his set of dos and don'ts. From the arrogance of the ignorant and from the ignorance of the uninformed zealot, Lord deliver us!

Vance is a highly successful businessman whom I met in some of my travels. He was an ardent Christian, open, friendly and generous; but he was hurting. He had supposed that his generalized anxiety sprang from the fact that his marriage was less than ideal, and that he didn't always feel loved by his children.

In a series of Primal Integration sessions he went back instantly to the death of his invalid mother when he was three or four years old. He relived his terrible sense of desolation when she died. There was a surrogate mother for a time who was very stern and unloving. Then his dog died, a major tragedy, for at that point he felt no one loved him but his dog. Then a good friend of his died. As he relived this period of his childhood, he said, with infinite sadness, "Everyone goes away and leaves me."

One might ask, since those things happened long ago, why dig them up and go through the pain of reliving them? The answer is that every experience, major or minor, has some effect upon the personality and the way we function. Childhood hurts, especially the deprivation of love, leave their mark. In the case of Vance, he was unconsciously trying to get his wife to meet his unmet childhood needs. His earnest religious faith had not eradicated his childhood pain, any more than it would have solved the problem of a diseased appendix. Vance wrote later that his primal experience had changed his life.

Faith of Your Parents

Assuming that you received some religious instruction as a child, is the religion of your childhood adequate for you now? Have you made it your own and expanded it, or is it still the faith of your parents?

Let's take a hypothetical situation in which you inherit a large furnished house where your deceased parents lived for many years. Circumstances require that you make this your home for the foreseeable future. You find that the house is furnished with a strange and unsatisfying mixture of Colonial, Danish Modern, early Salvation Army, and a wild assortment of many other kinds of furnishings. You find the mixture disturbing.

You try shifting it about, but this doesn't work. Finally you take it all out into the backyard and study it. This piece will do in the living room, and that one in the bedroom, another will do splendidly in a second bedroom, and so on. Finally you have your home about half furnished quite satisfactorily with inherited furniture. An assortment of odds and ends is left over. You call the Salvation Army or Goodwill and have them come for it. Then you go shopping for the additional pieces you will need to complete the job. Finally, it becomes *your* house, especially after you have done some painting and a bit of remodeling. It is no longer your parents' house; it is *yours*. So it is with the religion of our childhood. The fundamentals may all be there, but it is not truly yours until you reexamine it and, if necessary, alter it in the light of your own needs and experience.

Our son had moved away from home and after a time returned home for a visit and bought one of our cars. When I next visited him in Los Angeles I found he had had the car repainted, though it had a perfectly good paint job. "I had to do it, Dad, to make it my car instead of yours. I also added some accessories." I said, "Great! It surely doesn't look like my car (it was a vivid red). I'm glad you fixed it up just the way you like it and made it your own." Our religious faith, too, needs to be made our own.

There appears to be no direct correlation between orthodox belief and wholeness. Hosts of people believe all the right things without experiencing any sense of love, joy or peace, much less emotional maturity. Jesus did not urge his disciples to believe in a complicated set of doctrines. At one point he said, "Believe in God, believe also in me." [9] All the rest seemed to have to do with loving and obeying him.

A very able and dedicated Christian woman had become a kind of combination disciple, co-worker, traveling companion and assistant to one of America's outstanding religious leaders. This leader had a vast following around the world, and she made a number of trips overseas with him. After one such extended tour she said to me, with a deep sigh, "Saints are not easy to be with constantly. He's one of the greatest men in the world, and I love him dearly, but at times he is absolutely impossible." Was he a whole person?

Yes, of course. Was he perfect? No, not any more than was the Apostle Paul who couldn't get along with Barnabas; or Simon Peter who couldn't see eye to eye with Paul on theological matters.

Don't try, my friend, to be good, or perfect. You'll never make it. Just work toward becoming a whole person; and that is achieved through love.

5

Are You a Neurotic?

> ". . . Though the patient enters therapy insisting he wants to change, more often than not, what he really wants is to remain the same and to get the therapist to make him feel better. His goal is to become a more effective neurotic. . . . He prefers the security of known misery to the misery of unfamiliar insecurity."
> —Sheldon B. Kopp

Are you a neurotic? Well, you could have a neurotic trait or two without being labelled a neurotic. Many people have one or more neurotic traits, yet function normally in society. A standard definition of a neurotic is "an emotionally unstable individual," which is vastly different from having a few "peculiarities."

Howard Hughes appeared to have some startlingly neurotic traits, such as refusing to be seen in public and possessing an abnormal fear of touching any object which might carry germs. Was this billionaire an emotionally unstable individual? Many would classify him as a highly successful financial and industrial genius with some severe neurotic traits. (Immense wealth can get you certain privileges, such as having your neuroses labelled "interesting idiosyncrasies.")

J. Paul Getty, another billionaire, had an abnormal fear of flying and a horror of wasting money. Did the fact that he installed a pay telephone in his English mansion to keep guests from running up toll calls or his numerous unsuccessful marriages make him a neurotic?

Perhaps it would be fair to suggest that an individual who is functioning reasonably normally in society, despite a number of neurotic traits, would not necessarily be termed a true neurotic. On the other hand, a person who cannot hold a job, drinks to

excess, and alienates all of his associates could well fall into the
general category of an unstable personality.

A woman was leaving my office after the first of a series of counseling sessions. I said, "I want you to know that although you have
some serious personal difficulties, you are not a neurotic." She
brightened instantly and said, "Oh, thank you, thank you! I've been
beaten down so long by my husband that sometimes I don't even
know whether I'm totally sane." It is possible to lose one's identity
and perspective through constant criticism.

A neurotic is "a person who consistently over-reacts," according
to one somewhat over-simplified definition. For instance, anyone is
capable of being hurt by strong criticism. A person who consistently
bursts into tears, or goes into deep depression as the result of criticism, might be considered somewhat neurotic.

Even if, by stretching the definition, you should conclude that
you are a neurotic, it is encouraging to remember that a psychiatrist
wrote a book some years ago titled, "Be Glad You're a Neurotic."
His thesis was that some of the everyday neurotic traits common to
most of humankind can provide a stimulus for greater personal
growth.

Are "Workaholics" Neurotic?

I have been called a "workaholic" by some friends and associates.
Even my wife, in her loving and gentle way, has thrown in her lot
with these false accusers. I reply, somewhat defensively, that even if
it is a neurotic trait, at least it results in a lot of work getting done.
That's a poor rationalization, true though it may be. Let's see where
this type of neurotic trait originates.

My father, a bundle of vibrating, driving, energy—not always
well directed—thought me to be lazy because I didn't hoe weeds
with consumate zeal or milk the cows with gladness of heart. I
hated the farm with a passion and rejoiced with exceeding great
joy when it was sold and we moved to the city. But the damage was
done. I continued to see myself through my father's eyes—I was
lazy. On top of that, I was a victim of what I call the "run and get
me the hammer" syndrome. Many children suffer from this malady.
They are told to "run upstairs and get me. . . . Run and tell your
father. . . . Run and bring me. . . . Run . . . run . . . run." The
adults don't run, but the kid is supposed to become a joyous speed-
ing blur as he darts here and there on a thousand urgent errands.
So, as the result of being accused of laziness—the ultimate sin in my
father's eyes, plus spending my boyhood rushing hither, thither,
and yon in an effort to win parental approval, I became somewhat
of a compulsive worker.

Somewhat—that's the modifying word. A dedicated workaholic will seldom, if ever, take a vacation. He is so closely identified with his work that he feels he will have no identity if he is not busy. I happen to enjoy vacations and have used them to visit some sixty-five countries, some of them half-a-dozen times or more. So, I qualify only as a modest workaholic.

Yet, I plead guilty to possessing a neurotic trait. I work excessively at times, but I love it! As much as I enjoy fly fishing I usually derive more positive enjoyment from some things which have a higher priority—things which some people call *work*. Work is what you *have* to do. If you don't have to do it, it can be called pleasure.

Now, having purged my soul to some extent by an honest confession of a modest neurotic trait, complete with rationalization, let's move on and examine some important aspects of the neurotic personality.

It can be said that none of us is totally, completely, whole. Each of us fails in some degree to measure up to the standard. "For all alike have sinned, and are deprived of the divine splendour. . . ." [1] We each lack total maturity. We are not fully integrated. Any wholeness which exists in us is a matter of degree. Whether we use the term *sinner, neurotic, impaired personality, unstable,* or *emotionally immature,* we are talking about the same thing. How did we get this way?

The Origin of Neurosis

In his earlier writings Sigmund Freud held the opinion that neurosis originates as the result of some childhood trauma, which is primarily sexual in nature.

Somewhat later he expressed the belief that neurosis originates in the Oedipal conflict (the little girl's built-in desire to win her father; the small boy's drive to win his mother).

Still later he ascribed emotional and mental illness, and virtually all aberrant behavior, to conflict between the id and the superego—put simply, conflict between conscience and the pleasure principle.

Later on Freud came to see that since early environment played an enormous part in the creation of personality, rejecting parents were undoubtedly a primary or at least contributing cause of emotional instability. But toward the end of his life he came to the conclusion that there is probably no single specific cause for neurotic behavior, and he felt that there may well be a multiplicity of causes. This seems, to many modern psychologists, to be a very realistic view.

In this chapter, we are not dealing with emotional basketcases, but with people who are hurting to some degree emotionally, spiritually, and situationally. We are concerned not only with those individuals whose behavior and attitudes are destructive to themselves and others, but those who experience a lack of serenity and inner peace.

This might include, for example, a man who, in his compulsive pursuit of success, wealth, and recognition, neglects his family, as well as the person whose emotional distress results in one or more physical complaints.

Franklin is a good illustration of this type of neurotic behavior. His consuming ambition enabled him to become the president of a large national corporation. Like most people, he was a mixture of strengths and weaknesses. He was an able executive, a loyal church member, an avid reader of religious literature including the ancient mystics, and gave thirty percent of his income to church and charity. I knew him well and admired his many fine traits. Unfortunately, his excessive ambition made him difficult to get along with, and he had few friends. During his younger years he had an affair with his secretary. His wife found out about it and determined never to forgive him. She reminded him of it consistently. Though he knew all about divine forgiveness he could not forgive himself, and in a period of deep depression he attempted suicide. His inner tensions brought on a whole complex of physical symptoms which plagued him constantly. He ended his days virtually friendless, suffering acutely, and filled with remorse from which he could secure no release. He was basically a fine Christian man with many splendid traits, marred by a number of neurotic tendencies which limited his happiness and fulfillment.

Now let us consider a few common or garden varieties of everyday neurotics whom most of us encounter in the course of a lifetime:

Types of Neurotics

The FANATIC: Excessive enthusiasm marks the fanatic, together with an uncritical devotion to some cause, which is usually religious or political. Among these are the Neo-Nazis, the numerous revolutionary groups proliferating around the world, religious fanatics, social zealots who will cheerfully kill those who do not show enough compassion and social righteousness.

I recall a woman who made life miserable for her church for nearly ten years. She was a self-described "Bible-believing, born-again, all-out-for-the-Lord, dedicated worker in the Lord's vineyard"; which might have been all right except that she kept up a ten-year barrage of criticism of her church, its officers, teachers, and the minister. She boasted that she spent two to four hours a day on the telephone stirring interest in her crusade. She wore a grim smile, quoted Scripture by the ream, and directed a Bible class for women in a downtown building. She had ulcers, colitis, migraine headaches and sundry other assorted illnesses. Peace came to her church only when she moved away.

She was a bitter, vindictive, quarrelsome individual who made life miserable for many people, including herself. Like most fanatics she was convinced of the righteousness of her crusade. Her intense zeal, bolstered with Scripture quotations and pious phrases, initially won her a following until her devotees discovered the bitterness and hate behind her facade of piety.

Winston Churchill once said that "a fanatic is one who can't change his mind and won't change the subject," which is true enough, but a dedicated fanatic is somewhat more complex.

The GOSSIP: This social pest is "first with the worst," and derives infinite satisfaction from gathering and disseminating the latest titillating bits of information about people. Such a person gains a sense of power from collecting and passing on the latest rumors. The gossip-monger usually is a frustrated individual, and compensates for the lack of satisfaction by living vicariously through the lives of others.

A sexually frustrated woman can get a secondhand thrill by sharing news of the latest instance of illicit sexual activity in the community. A man frustrated in his desire to achieve success in some field can compensate by compiling bits of negative information about his peers and passing it on.

The PARANOID: The paranoid individual is emotionally very sick. A public health nurse consulted me about the fact that the Federal Drug Administration agents were listening in on her phone conversations, following her in their cars and spying on her at work. It took an hour for her to relate the multitudinous plots being hatched against her. Finally I asked her, "Are you taking any medication, prescription or otherwise?" She hesitated, then admitted that she was taking six to eight Dexamyl capsules a day and had been doing so for several years. I said, "You must be aware that amphetamines, of which Dexamyl is one, can trigger paranoia in many people." She nodded. "And," I added, "your dosage is enormous. You must have built up a substantial tolerance for it, but it's affecting your perception. Since you feel guilty about taking the drug, you imagine that the FDA is after you."

I was aware, of course, that it is impossible to talk a person out of paranoia, but I was interested clinically in discovering the extent of her obsession. I phoned the office of the Federal Drug Administration in San Francisco and told an agent that I was talking with a young woman who believed that she was being followed by FDA spies. He laughed, and said, "She's on "uppers," probably amphetamines. A week never passes but some joker dashes in here and shouts, 'Call off your men or I'm going to get you!' " I asked, "Would you be willing to tell this young woman that you are not interested in her case?" "Sure."

I asked her to take the phone, and he assured her that they were not interested in individual users of drugs, but only in pushers. She put down the receiver, looked at me suspiciously, and said, "You're in with them. It's all part of the plot." She left, and I never saw her again.

Paranoia has several stages, all a part of one emotion. At the first level one may be *overly-sensitive*. The next level finds a person *excessively* overly-sensitive. The third stage is *suspicion,* then *excessive* suspicion. We then reach the final stage, *persecution.* It may be the Russians, or just "them," out to get you. "They" are plotting against you.

Rabid right-wingers who fear a take-over by Blacks, Jews, or "them," are obviously paranoic. A crusader, marshalling some facts to which he adds suspicion and hate, will often attract a following of potential or actual paranoics.

Sometimes severe depression, or a sudden reaction to certain prescription drugs, or physical illness, can release some latent paranoia. While partially recovered from a period of deep depression, a counselee developed a full-blown case of paranoia. He was certain that his neighbors had his apartment bugged, that his phone was tapped, and that various people were plotting against him. When fully recovered from the depression and no longer taking medication his unfounded suspicions disappeared.

The OVERLY-COMPLIANT: The daughter of a wealthy couple, in her late twenties, was pretty, warm and friendly. She consulted me about her extreme overcompliance. Never having been allowed to make decisions for herself, or assume responsibilities of any kind, she found it almost impossible to stand up for herself. She could make decisions only after agonizing for hours or days. Although she no longer lived at home, her mother either visited or phoned her to discuss even the smallest decision. The confused young woman loved her mother, yet quietly resented her dominance. She was unsure about her rights as an adult.

Achieving emotional maturity and a sense of her own identity took time. We were working against more than twenty years of domination by an overprotective mother. But gradually she matured into a young woman able to make her own decisions.

The HARD-DRIVING BUSINESSPERSON, INCAPABLE OF MATURE LOVE: Leonard grew up in a home surrounded by an abundance of material possessions. His every wish was gratified. He received a surfeit of things, but no love. Both parents were obsessed with material values, and the mother, having divorced the father, succeeded in amassing great wealth. Leonard, a friendly extrovert, married an intelligent, but passive and dependent young woman, and proceeded to dominate her life for more than twenty years. She induced him to come in for counseling under the threat of divorce. Naturally he was uncooperative, having been forced into coming. They were from out of town and planned to spend two weeks of daily intensive counseling. On the fourth day Leonard received an urgent message, he said, requiring his presence in St. Louis for a business conference. He never returned.

His wife continued with the counseling over a period of several months. She discovered in time that during their entire marriage Leonard had been having serious affairs with an assortment of women. Eventually this formerly passive-dependent wife decided that she preferred to face life on her own, rather than live with a man alternately hostile and loving. When she told him of her decision he immediately moved in with one of his women friends. In his drive for financial success Leonard has never spent so much as an hour exploring his own personality, his motives, or his values. There was for him only one value: money and what it could buy.

The "LITTLE BOY" MAN: This is not a clear-cut neurosis, but it involves serious emotional immaturity. Ken was such a man. He came for counseling in a panic when his wife announced that she was getting a divorce and asked him to move out. Although he was reasonably successful in business, in our discussions he manifested all of the traits of an abandoned little boy. I could sense the anxiety generated in the home by this husband-father who sounded and acted so much like a petulant, demanding child. Ken was faithful about keeping his appointments until the divorce was final, whereupon he abruptly discontinued counseling. Obviously he had little interest in personal growth and sought only to keep coming in the hope that his wife would relent when she learned he was "trying."

The MASOCHIST: Masochism is usually defined as deriving "pleasure through pain" (from Leopold von Sacher-Massoch, whose sexual perversions involved gaining pleasure from pain being inflicted by a love object), but today the term *masochist* is more generally used to describe a person who unconsciously derives some morbid satisfaction from either pain, bad luck or disaster. Such individuals actually seem to invite disaster unconsciously. Among these are: the accident prone, trouble prone, sickness prone, and bad judgment prone.

Carl Gustav Jung comments on the fact that there are some people who seem to attract to themselves a disproportionate number of adverse circumstances, while certain other people draw to themselves an equally disproportionate number of "good things." He did not seek to explain this phenomenon, except to say that the better integrated a person is—that is, more whole—the more advantageous things one attracts, whereas the less whole a person is, the more "bad things" seem to befall him. It is almost as if one who is poorly integrated sets up a "force field" which invites negative things, whereas the whole, or well-integrated person, attracts "good things."

One man, who had managed to maintain a sense of humor despite a depressing childhood, said, "When I was a kid even the Good Humor Man used to yell at me, and when I went to a seminar on love, I got beaten up." These were exaggerations, of course, but evidence that one can endure misfortune and still manage to laugh about it.

Masochism is, in a sense, an emotion or the manifestation of one, a negative drive or force originating in great inner conflict and a weak self-image. A child who is unloved and berated learns to hate himself and often develops into an adult who manifests self-distrust, inferiority, or even self-loathing. Such a person does not feel worthy to succeed, and may, though no fault of his own, attract disaster, destructive relationships and consistent failure. This inner self-defeating force is one of the most difficult to eradicate. It seldom yields to positive thinking, exhortation, inspirational reading, or self-help. Deep, lengthy therapy is usually indicated. It doesn't seem fair or just—and it isn't—that a child becomes so damaged through no fault of his own that he ends up with self-hate and failure, yet it happens to millions of people.

The DOGMATIC LEGALISTIC AUTHORITARIAN: The roots of Helen's distress were so deeply buried that talking about it seemed futile, so we began a series of Primal Integration sessions. When regressed to childhood, in a score or more of two-hour sessions, she raged at her father, the pastor of a very legalistic church. I came to see him, through her, as rigid, unbending, terribly fearful of offending God, demanding, insecure and autocratic. The family moved every two or three years. The little girl, uprooted so often, found it difficult to make friends. She felt "different" and hated it. Her childhood bitterness and hostility had been repressed, and now in these sessions it came out in violent, explosive rages at her hostile and demanding father. The climax came when she relived the buried memory of being sexually molested by a devoted member of her father's church.

The dogmatic, authoritarian religionist is a very frightened person. In such a person what sounds like enormous zeal for God is composed largely of fanaticism and fear in about equal parts. Such people fear their emotions and dare not admit them into awareness. These people are veritable pressure cookers, ready to blow. They secure a little release by condemning any and all devia- tion from their own particular theological and moral code. Often they are sexually repressed and have neurotic and false ideas about the evils of the sex drive. Bury these legitimate God-given emo- tions of fear, sex, and anger and you get a fearsome mixture guaran- teed to distort any personality.

The SEXUALLY PROMISCUOUS: The sexually promiscuous individ- ual is seldom oversexed. One woman, typical of many, put it very well. "I don't particularly enjoy the sex act. I just want to be held, and I go through with the whole experience just to get that." What such a woman is after is a warm relationship with a man, rather than sex itself.

The wife of a prominent civic leader confessed ashamedly that she had had numerous furtive affairs with some of her husband's friends, despite the fact that she was sexually frigid. She had no idea why she seemed driven to do this, and she felt guilty and confused. I explained to her that an impaired relationship with her father drove her to seek an elusive acceptance by phantom father figures, but did not resolve the real problem. Ultimately, in some primal sessions, she was led back into childhood and relived the largely forgotten details of feeling rejected by her father and of being raped as a child. She had completely buried the traumatic sexual assault and relived it with intensity.

It was not just *understanding* the roots of her problem which helped her, but the *reliving* of the traumas. The nameless anxiety which drove her to become sexually promiscuous was discharged. Upon completing her therapy she and her husband learned to communicate for the first time and established a completely new relationship. She felt no need to fill him in on details of her pro- miscuity but did tell him about the sexual assault in childhood which had damaged her emotionally and sexually. She reported later that she was no longer sexually frigid.

The RESCUER: These people are highly praised for their unselfish devotion as they bustle about rescuing, helping, saving, serving, ministering. This is neurotic, of course, only when it becomes ex- cessive. The man who neglects his own home to paint and paper and tinker for the neighbors is a good illustration. Another is the woman whose own family—or health and normal self-interest—are neglected while she serves as the chairperson of seven committees and devotes every available hour to "doing good." Such persons with an excess of compassion for others while neglecting their own needs have a distorted sense of values.

Many pastors are caught up in this neurotic passion to save the world while wife, children and home life are neglected. Part of the problem lies in the real or imagined expectations of a congregation, whose unrealistic demands bear no relationship to the number of hours in a day or the available energy of a minister. Some of the difficulty lies with the minister who finds it impossible to balance both the legitimate needs of church and family. He cannot neglect his church responsibilities, yet trying to meet all of the expectations of the congregation may well result in impaired family relationships. From meeting with hundreds of pastors in conferences and retreats I can testify that theirs is not an easy dilemma to resolve; and forty years as a pastor makes me enormously sympathetic with the overworked minister and with his wife who is often uncertain whether to blame church, husband, herself or God.

There are scores of neurotic-type personalities, but perhaps we can lump a few more of them under several categories suggested by Virginia Satir, one of the founders of the Mental Research Institute in Palo Alto, California. In *Peoplemaking* [2] she suggests four main categories to which I have added two others. They are:

The DISTRACTOR: He can always change the subject—any subject, and usually turns the conversation back to himself.

The COMPUTER: This super-reasonable intellectualizer always has a word for it, usually a long one.

The PLACATOR: This one is always accommodating, and so sorry he's not perfect.

The BLAMER: Always secure in the knowledge that it is not his fault, he can show you that it is always your fault.

The ADVISOR: This character may not be able to solve the problem of his own personality distortions, but is always willing to advise you with your problems.

In addition to Virginia Satir's interesting list, I have added two more:

The BIBLE-TOTING, BIBLE-QUOTING NUISANCE: This is one who, with a sweet plastic smile and unctuous voice, provides a Scripture verse for every conceivable occasion, with the assurance that all you need to do is pray about it. This simplistic solution confuses the new Christian and irritates the more mature ones.

The YES-BUT'ER: This interesting individual will ask for your advice, but no matter what you suggest, he replies with, "Yes, but. . . . " The only effective response is to ask, "What are your alternatives?" This is not only a stopper, but is psychologically better than giving direct advice.

Another neurotic difficult to deal with is the compulsive talker. A Hindu proverb reads, "The miserable are very talkative." One way these people keep their inner distress partially out of awareness is by talking up a verbal storm. They are suffering from a vague, unacknowledged inner tension together with weak self-esteem. As long as they can hold your attention, and hear the sound of their own voice, the inner anxiety is temporarily allayed.

It has often been said that a neurotic builds air castles, the psychotic lives in them, and the psychiatrist collects the rent. This and a thousand other quips dealing with the emotionally disturbed are told in an effort to lessen our own anxiety, for we know at a deep level that none of us is free from some neurotic traits.

A great deal of emotional distress is caused by inability to accept one's sexual identity. Lenora is a case in point. Her marriage was seriously impaired by her emotional and sexual frigidity. In a seminar I was leading I sensed her enormous fear of something. When she signed up for a weekend primal session she found herself as a child experiencing some horror. She feared to look at it and wanted to end the experience. She was led gently and gradually to look at the horror. It turned out to be a little girl in a frilly dress, from which the young woman recoiled. She could not accept the idea of her femininity, which the frilly dress symbolized. As a little girl she had wanted to be a boy and totally rejected her own sexual identity in an effort to win her father's love and approval. Now she was face to face with the need to accept her identity as a girl-woman. It was a lengthy and difficult process, for she had spent a lifetime denying her feminine identity. Having lived with a false sexual identity for years, time and effort were required to resolve the problem, but in time she accomplished it.

The Inferiority Complex

Compensation is a device utilized to help us balance, for instance, inferiority feelings in one area, by achieving something significant in another. Alfred Adler, who coined the term inferiority complex, had a brother, George, who was out-going and socially very active, whereas Alfred was shy and retiring. Alfred compensated by achieving excellent grades—better than George's. Later, as a psychiatrist, he pronounced the basic human drive to be the struggle to compensate for feelings of inferiority or weakness. This is a legitimate device which we use almost automatically. Overcompensation, however, is a distortion.

A woman of considerable ability was chosen Secretary of the Month by the members of her local Secretary's Club. She then decided to become the most outstanding secretary in the State and managed to win that recognition. This fired her imagination. She decided to run for Mother of the Year in her State, and by electioneering and pressuring her friends and family, she managed to win that. A son said, "Mother will never be satisfied until she is All-American Mother of the Year, and then Mother of the Universe. Her neurotic ambition knows no bounds. She spends half her time running for office and honors, and the other half meddling in the affairs of her grown children." This is a clear-cut case of overcompensation for weak self-esteem. If you can get enough people to vote for you, or praise you, or notice you, it temporarily diminishes the buried self-hate. The feeling is, "If all these people praise me, or accept me, then I must be pretty okay!" But the weak ego is insatiable. It is never entirely satisfied with these tricks, because nothing fully contents it except the awareness that *you* accept yourself as an okay person regardless of what anyone else says or thinks.

There is an unavoidable tension within each of us, in need of being resolved. One voice says, "I am dust and ashes, one of four billion people on a tiny planet in a distant corner of the universe." Another voice says: "I am a child of the Eternal God, made in his image, deathless, immortal, loved by him as much as any human who has ever lived." The tension existing between these two equally valid truths can be resolved when we fully accept our humanity, with all its weaknesses, and our divinity as children of God. And the loving heavenly Father who created us for fellowship with himself knows and forgives all our human weaknesses. Despite our frailties as neurotics and sinners, he invites us to have fellowship with him, for he declares us to be worthy, whether we feel it or not.

6

Love, Marriage and Wholeness

> "People in love are under the influence of the most violent, most insane and most transient of passions. They are required to swear that they will remain in that excited, abnormal, exhausting condition until death do them part."
> —George Bernard Shaw

At a retreat a rather grim looking woman asked me in one session how much time I spent away from home. When I told her she said, with considerable asperity, "Well, I certainly wouldn't want to be married to *you*!" The bitter look on her face tempted me to say, "That's a mutual reaction," but I smiled and said, "That is an option not currently open to you; but my wife and I both think we have a splendid marriage."

Then I asked, "Are you happily married?"

"I'm divorced. He couldn't meet my needs."

The group was too large for us to go into the details, and I did not feel led to pursue the matter further, except to say, "We don't marry primarily so that we can spend our lives doing delightful things for this other person, meeting his or her needs, giving unlimited and unconditional love. We marry for largely self-centered reasons: to get our own needs met. When I meet this lovely creature and get to know her, being with her makes me feel so good, so wonderful in fact, that I want to feel this way for the rest of my life; so I say, 'Let's get married!' And if she feels this same ecstatic glow when she is with me and wants to feel that way the rest of her life, she will probably say, 'How soon?' "

This is not to say that unselfishness cannot exist in marriage. It can and must exist or the marriage will end in disaster. However, after the initial euphoria has diminished somewhat, we may begin to discover certain oddities, not to say peculiarities, in the personality of the one we have married.

We marry to get our needs met, to put it bluntly, and when the other person fails to satisfy them we are disillusioned, or hurt, or angry over having been betrayed. What has been betrayed, of course, is our unrealistic, pink euphoric dream of permanent marital bliss, now foundering on the shoals of "debt, dishes and diapers" as one puzzled wife expressed it.

Excessive Demands in Marriage

A woman with eighteen children, who entered Britain's Housewife of the Year contest, was invited to say what quality she most admired in a man. She said, "Moderation!" One can only speculate as to precisely what she had in mind, but moderation is a great boon to marriage. It is often the excessive demands or expectations that mar a relationship.

After several counseling sessions with a husband and wife, I said, "Both of you have some unmet needs, and undoubtedly some changes will have to be made on the part of both of you. But," speaking to the husband, "one thing stands out. You are making some excessive demands on your wife. Some of these, the unrealistic ones, are left over from childhood. They are needs your mother should have met but couldn't or didn't for some reason; and now you are trying to get your wife to meet both your adult needs, as well as a lot of childhood needs left over from the past."

He said, "I don't buy that. They all feel like adult needs." "Of course they do," I replied. "All of them feel like 'here and now' needs because we experience them in the present. But I can tell you dogmatically that neither your wife, nor any other woman I know of, can meet all of your needs, all of the time, because some of them are totally unreasonable." I explained what some of them were; but in his neurotic need to get all of his needs met, both past and present, he began to shop around for a counselor who would agree with him that his wife was being stubborn, selfish, and unreasonable. He had tried out three marriage counselors at last report without finding complete satisfaction.

Perhaps no two people ever define love similarly, partly because we experience it differently, and because the word has many different basic meanings. Plato said, "Love is a grave mental disease." In Romans 13:10 we read that, "Love is the fulfilling of the law." Lord Dewar said, "Love is an ocean of emotion entirely surrounded by expenses." Propertius wrote, "Everyone in love is blind."

Once it was an article of faith, and is still a strong belief in many quarters, that unselfish love, tenderness, devotion, sexual feelings, and eternal fidelity came along with the wedding cake. They don't. The euphoria and excitement of the courtship period are based on the hope—virtually a conviction—that the two people have finally found the love and romance for which they have always searched. But if the marriage is based on unrealistic expectations or bad judgment, it begins to flounder and the complaint is made that "the romance has gone out of our marriage."

Actually, it was not genuine romance in the first place, but a kind of unrealistic euphoria based on hope, expectation, and the initial excitement of believing that "all my needs will be met forever." Genuine romance is the result of the fusing of two lives after years of sharing themselves with each other mentally, emotionally and physically. The marriage is increasingly strengthened by a maturing sexual relationship.

Passive Husbands, Dominant Wives

One of the most common complaints I have heard in some forty years of counseling is the accusation made by wives that their husbands are not "dominant" (meaning strong, competent, and assured) ; and the criticism men make that their wives are "too dominant" (strong, nagging, demanding). With astonishing frequency strong women are attracted to more passive men, and passive men tend to seek out strong or dominant wives. Later both may object to the excessive dominance or passivity of the other. (There are exceptions, of course, but dominant mothers tend to produce dominant daughters and passive sons.)

The woman may be attracted by his gentleness, forgetting, or not knowing, that a woman's basic need is for a man who is both strong and gentle; so she fails to find the strength she desperately longs for. Besides, at a totally unconscious level she senses that she is more likely to get her way with a man who is easily influenced. She would never admit into consciousness the idea of her being dominant.

Or, as in the case of Helen, she may be repeating, unconsciously, a family pattern. Helen revealed in counseling that Mother "ran the show, and Daddy was passive. He was so warm and loving and gentle. I just adored him. I realize now that Mother pushed him around. She had to, because he was weak; but I saw only the loving, affectionate side of him." So Helen married a succession of four passive-dependent men, each of whom was, or became, an alcoholic. In each marriage she earned the living, or most of it, because she was a dynamic and talented person. However, she complained bitterly that "men are so weak."

Another variation is the woman whose father was excessively dominant, aggressive, or tyrannical. In an effort, conscious or unconscious, to avoid a repetition of such a relationship, she seeks out a quiet, passive man who will be the exact opposite of her father. Some daughters of rejecting fathers marry men like their fathers in a totally unconscious effort to work out the unsatisfactory relationship with a male.

"The nagging, aggressive woman is often unconsciously demanding that which she most fears. By irritating a man, making unreasonable demands and criticizing, she is really trying to evoke a dominant response by attacking him for his lack of virility. Her aggression is fulfilling a double purpose, both protecting her against male dominance and, at the same time, demanding it. . . . Very aggressive women have phantasies of extremely tough men, but marry compliant ones. Insecure, nonaggressive men demand extremely submissive feminine women and marry dominant ones. . . . Each is seeking in the other a quality which should have been developed within themselves and which they are frightened of manifesting. The insecure woman is fearful of her submissive side, and the insecure man of his dominant . . . aspect." [1]

How to Ruin a Marriage

Ann Landers's column once contained a letter from a man who wrote:

Dear Ann Landers:
Will you please publish my letter and recommend that it be printed and given free to every man who pays for his marriage license. Every one of these suggestions has been tested. They all work:
(1) Start off right by getting boiled to the eyeballs on your wedding day. Begin early—like before the ceremony. This will give the bride and her parents a preview of what is to come. By the time you stumble to the honeymoon bed you are sure to pass out colder than a mackerel.
(2) Immediately after you return to your job, let your wife know you enjoy stopping on your way home from work for a bit of good fellowship. This will not give her the crazy idea that she can count on you for supper at any set time. Let her know from the start that she should "cook flexible."
(3) Don't make any promises about going to church with her on Sunday. Play it by ear. If you make a commitment you'll have to live up to it. Tell her every Sunday morning according to how you feel. Then, if for some reason you aren't in shape and don't feel like going, she'll have no beef.
(4) Don't get involved in any long-winded "discussions." *Discussion* is just a polite word for argument. The man is supposed to wear the pants in the family, and if you start off by letting your wife know it you'll save yourself a lot of trouble.

I know all these pointers are good because they worked for me. I was married to one of the sweetest girls in the world. She left me after she couldn't take it any more. I hope you will print this letter for other stupid fools like me. It took six months before I was willing to admit that my marriage failed for the reasons mentioned here. Being alone is hell.

One Who Knows

Ann Landers's reply:

Dear One:
    Your O. Henry ending is a gasser. Thanks for giving us the benefit of your Home Research. Are you listening, students?

It is tragic that so often our wisdom is purchased at so great a cost in terms of heartache and tears.

Marital Infidelity

One expects, realistically, that there will be a certain amount of marital infidelity among the married population at large; but something that is seldom discussed openly is the significant number of church members whose marriages have been blighted by extramarital affairs. My information is based on the very large number of erring husbands and wives with whom I have counseled over the years, who were church members in good standing, Sunday school teachers and church officers. A profession of faith and active membership in a church is no guarantee of marital fidelity.

I would not label these people as *hypocrites,* a very judgmental word. The only ones whom Jesus labelled hypocrites were the very moral Pharisees, who tithed and obeyed the letter of the law, but neglected "the weightier matters of the Law, justice, mercy, and good faith." [2]

One could say of these unfaithful husbands and wives that they are weak, or foolish; but when I get to know all of the circumstances involved—the individual's childhood background, all of the facts about the marriage—I never feel judgmental, but rather a sense of concern and compassion. When Jesus dealt with adultery he neither condemned nor condoned, but accepted the erring individual.

Surveys have shown that half of married men and a quarter of married women commit adultery. Dr. David R. Mace, professor of sociology at the Bowman-Gray Medical School, University of California, divides the unfaithful in marriage into five different types:

(1) The LIBERTINE. This individual seems to be unsuited to a

close, intimate, personal relationship and seems addicted to the idea of sexual variation.

(2) The BORED. For these people marriage has become dull, repetitive, and lacks stimulation. They seek excitement or another outlet.

(3) The CURIOUS. They want to act out sexual fantasies which almost everyone entertains.

(4) The EMOTIONALLY INSECURE. These immature persons are seeking to compensate for their insecurity and feelings of inadequacy. Often their basic motivation is not sexual, but rather a search for power and achievement, and the assurance that they are loved.

(5) The SEXUALLY FRUSTRATED. They respond to immediate erotic stimulation.

There are undoubtedly other causes as well. Many people enter marriage with the mistaken idea that once you find the right marriage partner, life will be lived thereafter on cloud nine. When they discover that marriage is not a continual state of bliss and contentment, they sometimes seek release and satisfaction outside of marriage. They may search for the "right partner." They are looking for the illusion of an idyllic relationship. This type of fantasy is based upon the false idea that there is such a thing as a perfect marriage partner and a perfect marriage.

Another factor is that when demands and expectations are met with disappointment, the partners may begin to feel unloved, and seek emotional and sexual satisfaction elsewhere.

In a substantial number of instances I have found that when one mate strays, the other very often seeks revenge for the real or imagined unfaithfulness. "If he can do it, so can I!" This provides an opportunity not only to "get even," but seeming justification for a partly unconscious urge to experiment, and kick over the traces.

What Is This Thing Called Love?

Judith Vorst defines it, tongue in cheek: "Love is much nicer to be in than an automobile accident, a tight girdle, a higher tax bracket or a holding pattern over Philadelphia. But not if he doesn't love you back.

"QUESTION: What is the difference between infatuation and love?

"ANSWER: Infatuation is when you think he's as sexy as Robert Redford, as smart as Henry Kissinger, as noble as Ralph Nader, as funny as Woody Allen, and as athletic as Jimmy Connors. Love is when you realize that he's as sexy as Woody Allen, as smart as Jimmy Connors, as funny as Ralph Nader, as athletic as Henry

Kissinger and nothing like Robert Redford—but you'll take him anyway." [3]

The Great Need for Affirmation

It will always remain a mystery why some people marry whom they do, for some couples seem so disparate, so totally unfitted to each other; but *why* we marry is not so complex. Ford Maddox Ford, quoted by Columnist Charles McCabe wrote that, "There is no man who loves a woman who does not desire to come to her for the renewal of his courage, for the cutting assunder of his difficulties. . . . We are all so afraid, we are all so alone, we all so need from the outside the assurance of our own worthiness to exist.

"To be assured of your worth, in a lonely and uncaring world, is maybe what it's all about. And this requires that your woman approve of you. This is an extraordinarily easy thing for most women to do. Partly, of course, this is from illusion—the lady does not wish to admit that she could have made a poor choice. But there is more than that. Women seem to possess a natural allegiance to the men they have thrown their lot with." [4]

A woman needs to be affirmed and reassured no less than a man. There are, of course, exceptions, but in general it can be said that a man wishes to be assured of his worth by being recognized for what he has achieved, for his accomplishments—that he is clever, or directs his corporation brilliantly, or makes a good score on the golf course. A woman desires to be recognized for her accomplishments, too, but she is much more anxious to be affirmed for the kind of person she *is,* and for her appearance. That she is lovely or beautiful, charming or talented, is usually of primary importance, while what she has produced—a good dinner, a nice painting, a lovely garden—looms as secondary in importance, though surely to be ignored at great cost.

Another very great need of wives is for affection without sex. A typical wife wants not *only* sexual activity as a physical-emotional-spiritual fulfillment, but she also needs affection—frequently expressed—which does not lead to sex. This factor is greatly ignored by the average husband.

A San Antonio, Texas, wife filed for divorce stating that her husband was a bore. The judge, thinking this hardly sufficient grounds for divorce, asked, "Just what is a bore?" She thought about it for a minute, then quoted, "A bore is a person who deprives you of solitude without providing you with company." The divorce was granted. Boredom afflicts a vast number of marriages.

A very frequent complaint of wives is that their husbands are uncommunicative. A typical wife may want companionship, conversation, and dinner out. What she may get is a short answer and a weekend of TV sports.

Schizoids (Intellectualizers) Fear Their Emotions

Another variation is the man (and there are some women like this) who are called schizoid personalities by psychiatrists. These people, says Anthony Storr, "endeavor to maintain their relationships upon a superficial level, or else withdraw from human contact altogether into an ivory tower of isolation which they defend against love as well as hate, since these two emotions are, for them, undifferentiated. . . . Schizoid people of high intelligence often achieve considerable success in the pursuit of power or in the fields of artistic or scientific endeavor. Their detachment from human relationships makes it possible for them to pursue intellectual avocations with the same intensity that more ordinary persons give to the pursuit of love. An air of superiority, so often assumed by schizoid individuals, is not endearing to the average person who seeks warmth and comfort from other human beings; and while schizoid people may be admired and respected, they are seldom regarded as loveable. . . . A mask of superior detachment conceals an overwhelming hunger for affections." [5]

One is not whole in any sense who cannot give and receive love; but very often an individual has been reared by undemonstrative parents and ends up overintellectualized and underdeveloped in terms of ability to express feelings. A person so limited cannot be "talked into" being more demonstrative; he is simply incapable of emerging from the cold gray castle of his lonely isolation. As a child he had to build his defenses in order to survive; to emerge now would require the demolition of his defense system, into which he has poured so much of his psychic energy.

It is not only husbands who are deficient in communicating. Writing to columnist Abigail Van Buren, one husband complained:

Dear Abby: Perhaps mine is a unique problem. . . . My wife complains constantly that I never do anything around the house. She says, "The people next door work together painting, gardening, etc., and their place looks great. You never do anything around here, and our place looks like a dump. All you want to do is play golf, or bring home extra work from the office."

She is right. But the reason I never do anything around the house is this: I once brought some paint home to paint a room, and she criticized the color. I started to work in the yard and she said, "Quit that, you're making a mess!"

Frankly, no matter what I do she finds fault with it. The golf course is pleasant and quiet. And when I am doing work I bring home from the office, at least she doesn't yell at me.

I have complimented her on her cooking, the way she looks, her housekeeping and everything I can think of, but she never even says, "Thanks." There must be other readers who could improve their family relations immensely by just learning to express a little warm, sincere appreciation. Thanks.

A Golf Widow's Golfer

Abby responded:

I score your advice a birdie after a good recovery from a common marital trap.

Marriage Counseling Is Not Magic

The nagging, unappreciative wife, the uncommunicative husband—there are a thousand variations. Each feels so lonely or unappreciated or unloved; each needs desperately to be affirmed and cared for. Many couples who come to our counseling center [6] expect some simplistic answers which will, in a session or two, or a month at the outside, solve the problem (straighten the other person out) and get the marriage back on the track. Experience shows that effective marriage counseling may require anywhere from three months to three years; for at the root of most marital problems are personality problems. When these personality malfunctions or abberrations are serious, many hours are required to resolve the difficulty. The marital conflict is often only a symptom of either a personality defect or a serious misunderstanding of what is involved in marriage.

One psychiatrist has said that the ideal marriage would be "two people who don't need each other." An individual who has vast needs and expects someone to fulfill them is often so preoccupied with these needs that he or she has no time or psychic energy with which to meet the needs of the other.

Many Teenage Marriages Fail

Teenage marriages are especially likely to end in disaster, chiefly because the immature youngsters have not lived long enough to know how to establish mature relationships. Statistics from the National Center for Health reveal that 54 percent of teenage marriages end in divorce; 36 percent are divorced when only the bride is a teenager; and 18 percent end in divorce when both bride and groom are twenty or older. The United States Department of Health, Education and Welfare reports that nearly half of all teenage marriages involve premarital pregnancy. An important factor is that quite often the marriage takes place more because of the pregnancy than because the couple has planned to be married.

Twelve Approaches That Won't Work

Dr. W. W. Broadbent, professor of psychiatry at the University of Southern California Medical Center in Los Angeles, names twelve approaches that won't work in giving and receiving love. He lists them as:

Seductive Woman: She uses the come-hither glance, the provocative dress, the touching, the soft voice. Her message is, "tell me I'm desirable."

Man's Man: He suffers from a case of terminal masculinity. He seldom smiles and never cries. His message is sent with a crushing handshake, a slap on the shoulder. It says, "I don't want anybody to have any of the doubts about my manhood that I have, so be a little afraid of me." He has to learn that there can be respect without fear.

Chameleon: This person always tries to find out what is expected and then complies in order to be accepted.

Saint: Can't you see how sweet I am, how understanding! The extra message is, "How could you reject anyone as loving and nonjudgmental as I am?" The saint may be hiding a devilish anger or judgments totally beyond the person's awareness.

Martyr: He or she may say, "Look at what I've done for you, and what do I get in return? Absolutely nothing." The message is "feel guilty, give me sympathy, and do what I want you to do!"

Fan style: This person frequently pours piles of syrupy praise on some individual while in the presence of others. The message: "You can't escape loving me. I've trapped you in my fusillade of accolades. How can you not admire someone who admires you?"

Nice Guy: He always has the same nice face, nice smile, and the same charming manner. Message: "How could you help liking a nice guy like me?" The nice guy is not always so nice at home—he vents his suppressed and repressed feelings on his family.

Dig Me: He is addicted to the double entendre. He mimics, jokes and translates the laughter of others into love for himself. Message: "I'm selling you barrels of laughs for just a cup of love. Now don't you at least like me?"

One-Upsman: He tries to show his mind is quicker and better than someone else's by making the person appear ridiculous. He always gets in the last word. Message: "Admire me for my cleverness in putting someone down."

Moralizer Style: The person says, "All my thoughts are virtuous, patriotic and righteous, and I want you to know it." But the extra message is, "If my wonderful goodness doesn't make you love me, then shame on you." This person lives in a world of "shoulds."

Frightened Fawn in the Forest: This one sends you the message that she is weak, delicate, defenseless, frightened. What she wants is to tether herself to a protector, a supporter.

Modesty Ritual: Play this role and you never have to admit to anyone how inadequate you really believe you are, nor the degree of esteem you may feel for yourself. You always underplay compliments, even by lying if necessary. The message: "I'm afraid to be a totally honest, separate individual. I'm trying to hide my feelings." [7]

Love—The Universal Need

Every human, however vehemently he may deny it, wants to be accepted, loved, admired, affirmed. The urge is universal, and nothing we do can totally conceal this deep human need. The important thing is to be honest with ourselves, with God, and with at least one other person. Failure to be honest results in a distortion of one's personality, which in turn distorts relationships. It is impossible to understand ourselves in isolation. We need to have our feelings and ideas mirrored back to us by loving, honest persons who care for us. This can often be accomplished best in a sharing group. In another chapter such groups are described in some detail.

One important kind of love is that which exists between parent and child. Sometimes this love which ideally should bind parent and child together in warm affection is marred and distorted.

Bernice, a dynamic woman of sixty-two, shared with me her discovery that love cannot be forced. "When I was two years old my father abandoned the family. Mother, with a whole batch of kids, had to go to work in a box factory to feed and cloth us. Our father never contributed a dime to our support. I grew to hate him.

"Years later, I happened to meet him and we established a fairly good relationship, though I had difficulty understanding or forgiving his failure to care for us. He has always been a boozer, drinking steadily throughout the day though never drunk. He was ninety when it appeared that I would be the one to take care of him. I decided, two years ago, to write and invite him to come and live with me. But I was having mixed feelings. His steady drinking, his foul-smelling cigars, and the fact of my resentment toward him stopped me cold. I felt I was supposed to love him, and felt guilty because I couldn't.

"You may recall," she continued, "that I shared this with you two or three years ago, and you said that I was under no obligation to feel affection for him, only *agape*-love, a kind of unconditional positive regard for him as a human being. That relieved my guilt over not "honoring" my father, which I took for some reason to mean that I had to love him, that is, feel affection for him. As soon as I learned that I didn't have to feel any particular filial affection for him, I felt released. Soon thereafter I wrote and invited him to come and live with me. I felt good about it. I knew I could handle it without any difficulty. Then, he discovered that my brother had a cabin on the coast where he could live, and he decided to go live there. It's wonderful how it worked out. I got the release from my guilt, and felt okay about having him live with me; then I was relieved to find he wasn't coming after all. He died recently, and for some strange reason I feel a sense of loss. He was a rotten father, but somehow I miss him." I told her that hers was the kind of love spoken of in 1 Corinthians 13, NEB, especially the part which reads, "Love keeps no score of wrongs; does not gloat over other mens' sins. . . . There is nothing love cannot face; there is no limit to its faith, its hope, and its endurance."

Acceptors and Rejectors

Dr. Daniel Casriel, author of *A Scream Away from Happiness*,[8] describes two basic types of persons whom he labels Acceptors and Rejectors, both of whom have difficulty in love relationships. The Acceptor is one who has learned early in childhood to pay a high price for love, in terms of pain or rejection. He fully expects to pay for any love he receives. The Acceptor is so accustomed to pain in a relationship that he comes to expect it. Although such a person will find it painful, he will take the hurt for granted and put up with it. He will often be immobilized by fear, and be only partially aware of the deep anger over being misused. Such people always have a low self-esteem originating in childhood deprivation.

The Rejector, with a much stronger self-esteem, tends to be less trusting in human relations, and turns off his pain, or covers it up. Even in a good marriage the Rejector feels lonely and isolated, having repressed not only pain but most of his other feelings. He does not allow himself to feel his inner suffering, but neither can he feel love.

The personalities of both Acceptor and Rejector were formed in childhood in reaction to the environment—mother, father, peers, life in general—and the individual so formed will always react to people in the same way. Exhortation, reading, advice, criticism, will have no effect. The personality reacts in the only way it knows how. Any change will take place only as the result of (a) a crisis, and/or (b) intense and prolonged therapy, (c) a sharing group, (d) a genuine conversion experience, or (e) a series of Primal Integration sessions. No one can predict in a given instance which will be the most effective.

Giving and receiving love is not easy if one has been conditioned in childhood to mistrust love; but it is worth whatever it costs in terms of time and effort to achieve this most important of all qualities.

The Nontoucher

A minister said recently, "I have preached perhaps a hundred sermons on love, and I thought I loved, although I have been told that I seemed rather distant and cold in my relationships. I could not touch another person, and of course didn't want to be touched. I knew I lacked something, and after a series of primal sessions [9] I discovered my buried capacity for love. What a change! Now I can not only touch people, I can hug them, and I feel far more warmth in all my relationships. This was achieved by reliving a lot of childhood hurts. This experience discharged most of the fear which had inhibited me all of my life. It is the most important thing that ever happened to me."

7

Aging, Death and Immortality

"I don't feel like an *old* man; I feel
like a *young* man with something
wrong with him."
   —an eighty-nine-year-old minister

Even if the thought of growing old and of dying, depresses you,
perhaps you should read this chapter, because ignoring these in-
exorable, if disheartening, facts of life is no solution. Face them
and you will handle them better when they arrive.

When Robert Browning wrote, in his own aging exuberance,

> Grow old along with me!
> The best is yet to be,
> The last of life, for which the first was made.
> Our times are in his hand.[1]

he was not merely whistling in the gathering gloom of advancing
years to keep up his spirits. Millions of senior citizens are having
more fun and fulfillment than they did thirty years earlier, and
many creative people have done their best work after the fictitious
"age of retirement."

For instance, Immanual Kant wrote his best philosophical works
at the age of seventy-four. Verdi composed his *Ave Maria* when
he was eighty-five. Goethe wrote *Faust* at age ninety. Michaelangelo
completed his greatest work of art at eighty-seven. Titian painted
his famous *Battle of Lepanto* when he was ninety-eight. Justice
Oliver Wendell Holmes set down some of his most brilliant legal
opinions at age ninety, and Tennyson wrote "Crossing the Bar"
when he was eighty.

Marc Chagall, still hale and hearty at eighty-nine, was seventy-
nine years old when he produced the two murals for the Metro-
politan Opera. Comedian George Burns won an Oscar at eighty.
At eighty-nine, pianist Arthur Rubenstein, though he could not

see the keyboard, played brilliantly from memory at Carnegie Hall. Adding to the list of star performers of the Geritol set, Jomo Kenyatta, who does not have the faintest idea how old he is, was at least seventy when he became president of Kenya. And Eamon de Valera served as president of the Republic of Ireland until 1973 when he was an amazing ninety-one years old.

Old Age Makes Us "More So"

Studies have shown that age does little for us except to make us "more so." A San Francisco Bay Area study of 140 older people revealed that there is little difference between the way a person reacts to life at seventy or thirty. "If people were worried about their health at age thirty, they stayed worried throughout their seventies; and if they were independent strivers when they were young, they are still go-getters at seventy," according to Dr. Joseph Kuypers, one of those conducting the study. "People continued on for better or worse without any radical transformation throughout old age," Kuypers continued. "For instance, a seventy-year-old woman who was hesitant, worrisome, had little faith in herself and seemed a stay-at-home, acted the same way when she was thirty-years-old. . . . Old age is not some kind of disease or the end of the road, but a continuation of what has been."

It was a man in his fifties who said, "Middle-age is that time of life when you're pushed around by two little voices, one saying, 'Why not?' and the other saying, 'Why bother?'" That may have been his experience, but my personal observation of aging people, and numerous scientific studies, tend to confirm the following ideas:

Your I.Q. Can Increase with Age

Although brain cells die at the rate of one hundred thousand per day by age sixty (there are roughly 15 million to start with), and though these cells are never replaced, one's I.Q. actually seems to increase with age. Psychologist Jon Kangas, director of the University of Santa Clara Counseling Center, found that the I.Q.'s of forty-eight men and women went up about twenty points between childhood and early middle age. When first tested as school children, members of the group had an average I.Q. of 110.7. In ten years this rose to 113.3, and by the time the subjects were in the 39–44 age group, the mean I.Q. was 130.1. The aging process need not mean a loss of intelligence.

Middle-aged and older people often have more energy than when they were young. One aging man said, "Old people don't get tired; it's the young who tire most. Confusion exhausts them. I've got more energy now than when I was younger because I know exactly what I want to do." And Columnist Charles McCabe of the *San Francisco Chronicle* speaks for many older people when he writes: "I have spent a great deal of my life in a state of almost total confusion. It was not until I was well into my forties that I found work that satisfied me. When I found that what I was doing was just exactly what I wanted to do, my physical and mental condition began to improve greatly."

That has been my experience. I have been a member of the trifocal chapter of the Social Security Club for seven years, working eight hours or more a day, six days a week, and in addition writing a book every year or so, supervising an organization that provides spiritual growth inventories for some five thousand persons a year, making two trips abroad annually, reading a vast deal, and with more energy than I had thirty years ago. Advancing years do not necessarily involve a decrease in physical and mental activity. If you have been brainwashed by the wretched myth that senior citizens are condemned to golf, gossip and geritol, and retire to their rocking chairs to prepare for an early onslaught of senility, that is probably what will happen to you. This is called a self-fulfilling prophecy.

Retirement Can Be Great If . . .

Once in the Far East a whimsical American pointed to a large group of tourists, all women, and said: "That's a Charliewood group." I asked what in the world a Charliewood group was. He replied, "It's not spelled like you think. It's a group of women murmuring to themselves, 'Charlie would have loved this. But Charlie died early of too much work and too little recreation.'" This man was about seventy-five and said he started traveling and enjoying life in his early fifties. "This way I can take my wife along, instead of having her live it up on my life insurance." He grinned and moved on.

It was an older person who still possessed a riotous sense of humor who first said, "Death is nature's way of reminding you to slow down." I went to an older physician who had retired some years previously but, feeling bored by inactivity he had re-opened his office and resumed his practice. I had not seen him in several years, and said, "You're looking well." He was silent for a moment as he continued to poke me here and there. Finally, he said, "You know, there are three ages of man—youth, middle-age, and . . . *you're* looking well." He had lost none of his sly humor, though he was in his eighties.

But a vigorous and fulfilling old age does not fall, like ripe fruit from a tree; it must be planned for. The tragedy is that the average person makes few if any specific plans for retirement. I have seen a number of dynamic industrialists who were running vast business enterprises up to the day of retirement, who, a few days or weeks later were looking bewildered and aggrieved. Several of them who were in vigorous good health at age sixty-five lived only a few short years thereafter. They were killed by inactivity, boredom and a sense of lost identity.

Women live an average of seven to nine years longer than men. At a time when a typical male is having added responsibility given him, with additional pressure, his wife is usually experiencing a lessening of stress. Children are now grown and have left home. Most women had more pressure-filled hours in their younger days, but less as they reach the middle years and beyond, accounting in part for their greater longevity.

Finding something that you really want to do, which gives you satisfaction and fulfillment, can make a vast deal of difference in *how fast you age.* It is now firmly established that stress is the great enemy; and this may come about because of having to work at a job that is unfulfilling, or as the result of too much pressure, an unhappy home situation, or generalized anxiety.

Living with Hope Instead of Anxiety

At age seventy-five the Japanese artist Hokusai was still enjoying passionately what he was doing. He wrote: "From the age of six I had a mania for drawing. . . . By the time I was fifty I had published an infinity of designs; but all I produced before seventy is not worth taking into account. At seventy-three I learned a little about the real structure of nature, of animals, plants, birds, fishes.

"In consequence, when I am eighty, I shall have made still more progress; at ninety I shall penetrate the mystery of things; at one hundred I shall certainly have reached a marvelous stage; and when I am one hundred ten everything I do, be it but a dot, will be alive. I beg those who live as long as I do to see if I do not keep my word." [2]

The monthly bulletin of a ministers' retirement fund told of a ninety-eight-year-old pensioner who said his happiness in retirement was based on "being as curious as a stray cat in a strange warehouse." The bulletin pointed out that a lively curiosity—an eagerness to learn—was a quality most of us in our childhood relied on to find out about the world. Through it we did such things as climb trees, learn where the berries were ripe, discover what was inside a clock. Those who retain an open-eyed sense of wonder and appreciation will never grow old mentally. They will stay *alive* all their lives.

There are as many jokes dealing with aging as there are about mothers-in-law. Perhaps, as with most humor, this is an effort to relieve our anxiety. A retired man once said that the difference between *good-looking* and *looking good* is about thirty years. Then, still dealing facetiously with the age factor, he added, "Just when you think you're over the hump, you find you're over the hill." Being able to joke about our problems, real or imaginary, is good therapy; and I notice that there appears to be no lessening of a sense of humor as people age. If anything, the witty get wittier, but it is conversely true that soured younger people become even more embittered as they age. Age simply intensifies your basic personality traits.

The myth persists that many people of advanced years are sick, fragile, and disabled. Recent studies have shown that only 10 percent of people over sixty-five are confined in any serious way. An even smaller proportion needs any unusual attention. Only 5 percent of this age group live in an institution.

New Discoveries About Aging

In his challenging book *A Good Age*,[3] Alex Comfort attacks *ageism*—prejudice against the elderly. "After all," he writes, "the elderly are the only outcast group that everyone eventually expects to join. I wonder what Archie Bunker would say about Puerto Ricans if he knew he was going to be one on his next birthday." Comfort points out that though the elderly are more prone to chronic diseases, they get fewer acute illnesses than the general population. Only 1 percent of the elderly can expect to become demented. "The human brain," Alex Comfort asserts, "does not shrink, wilt, perish or deteriorate with age." The one hundred thousand brain cells which are lost daily Comfort calls a "programmed clearing-out process" of the brain.

A woman waiting in a dentist's office glanced over the diplomas hanging on the wall. One bore the name of a boy with whom she had gone to high school in that city fifty years before. Later, in the dental chair, she looked at the dentist's deeply lined face, bald head, and stooped shoulders, and sensed that this could not be one of her classmates.

"Where did you grow up?" she asked.

"Right here."

"When did you graduate from high school?"

"In 1928."

"Really! Then you were in my class," she exclaimed.

"Oh? What did you teach?"

This story illustrates the fact that our minds do not age, that one can still feel thirty-five mentally at seventy, and be greatly surprised at "how old everyone looks" at a class reunion.

After a funeral several friends of the deceased who had acted as pallbearers were talking about their departed friend. One asked, "How much did he leave?" After a moment's silence someone said, "*All* of it." We all know intellectually that we are going to leave it all when we "shuffle off this mortal coil"; but emotionally there is often a tendency to cling to money, or familiar surroundings, to whatever gives us a sense of security. Many older people cling to their old homes, friends, and church, or club memberships. Others, who seem more adaptable, and who make friends easily, move to new areas where life may be more agreeable and less expensive.

I would like to pass on some of the findings of social scientists who have studied the aging process and a few of my own personal observations.

(1) If you have been success-motivated, an achiever, and/or compulsive worker, I would warn you about the fallacy of fighting battles you've already won. Charlie Bower tells of an acquaintance who was "one of those men who struggle for success long after they have it, who are still making touchdowns when the stands are empty, the other team long gone, and the shadows lengthening toward them. Like most of us, he was seeking happiness and was baffled that success had not brought it. But success itself is a sort of failure. You reach the end of the rainbow, and there's no pot of gold. You get your castle in Spain, and there's no plumbing." [4] It's important to recognize that success is an *inner* thing, rather than a matter of money, titles, and honors.

(2) Start planning for retirement five to ten years in advance. But vaguely expecting to buy a mobile home and go to live in Florida is not planning; nor does talking of purchasing a cabin "somewhere in the woods" constitute a plan. It takes careful thought and study, with some scouting, perhaps, to check out post-retirement places to live and the things you would enjoy doing. Don't expect golfing or fishing to be endless fun; or knitting, reading, and tending grandchildren. These things can become boring for people who have spent forty or fifty years in active pursuits.

(3) Get involved in church or community activities and volunteer work. There are countless opportunities to make your life count: ministering to shut-ins, the handicapped, the bereaved, those in need of transportation—the list is endless. Many cities have volunteer bureaus where one can register for varied types of service and

most churches can provide a list of creative and helpful activities. By all means, *get involved*. Do it, not only for the sake of those who are worse off than you, but for yourself as well, for it is more blessed to give than to receive, in the sense that the giver derives a greater blessing than the recipient.

Those Later Years Can Be Productive

Dr. Ben Duggar, a botany professor at the University of Wisconsin, was told at the age of seventy that he was through. He insisted that he was physically and mentally vigorous, but the faculty adhered to the rigid rule: at seventy you are finished.

Some of Duggar's graduates were at the Lederle Laboratories, the pharmaceutical house. Learning of his forced retirement they spoke to the management about their "old" prof. He was finally hired as a consultant to do independent research.

Lederle believed that the cures for most diseases might be found in the earth, and there were six thousand drawers with samples of mold to be investigated. Ben Duggar went to work. For a year or two there were no results. But when he was seventy-three he looked into one of the flasks and saw a golden mold. He isolated an antibiotic and gave it the name of "auremycin." The discoverer lived to see it cure or control more than fifty serious maladies.

But Ben wasn't finished. From that start he went on to discover another antibiotic—tetracycline, the most widely prescribed broad-spectrum antibiotic in the world. It is used to control, among other things, streptococcus, pneumonia, staphylococcus, typhus, and syphilis. Ben Duggar lived to be eighty-four, and of him it is said that he may have saved more lives than any physician in history. He had retired to fulfillment.

How long will you live? Statistically it depends somewhat on your profession, where you live, and how much stress you have lived under. Prosperous and scientifically advanced United States ranks twenty-fourth for men and ninth for women in life expectancy. American men live an average of 67.1 years, women 74.6 years.

Clergymen, scientists and teachers live longer than the average. Supreme Court Justices are long-lived, while journalists have a mortality rate almost twice as high as others listed in *Who's Who*.

Whatever their profession, people tend to live longer if they are permitted to work beyond the age of sixty or sixty-five, or if they find some creative and fulfilling activities after retirement. The Institute of Gerontology states that man could live longer if he were allowed to work longer, yet the trend in the United States is toward earlier retirement.

Facing Death Realistically

There is no guarantee that you will survive to old age, for accidents and disease take their toll of younger people, too. But it is an absolute certainty that you are going to die sometime.

Many euphemisms are employed to make the idea of death less threatening, such as "passed on," "with the Lord," "entered into rest," "gone to his (or her) reward," "no longer with us," "safe in the arms of Jesus," and sundry others. There is no need to disparage these little evasions, for death can strike a devastating blow, and whatever can be done to lessen the impact seems desirable. But the stark reality is that death comes to everyone. Like cancer—which people once could not talk about and, if so, only in whispers—the subject of death is one often avoided. (We often conceal our anxiety with humor, such as the comment that while nothing is certain except death and taxes, death doesn't get worse every time congress meets.) But in recent years numerous books and articles have been written and studies made that deal realistically with the theme of death. It is high time to open up for free and uninhibited discussion a subject which concerns every human.

For a time one of the major airlines experimented with a closed circuit TV which would enable passengers to view their take-off and landing on a television screen. It apparently met with a monumental lack of interest, for it was rather speedily abandoned. As one sweaty-palms traveler said, "If God had meant for us to see our take-off and landing, he would have put holes in the bottom of planes."

In the same vein, if God had thought that it would be of benefit to us he would have given us the ability to foresee the future, including the time and manner of our departure from this particular planet. I think I would just as soon not know, for I doubt if it would contribute anything to my peace of mind.

Psychiatrist Elizabeth Kübler-Ross has made an exhaustive study of death and the way people react to it. In an interview with Daniel Goleman [5] she pointed out that after the death of a loved one, when they come out of the initial shock, family members experience grief, "but with the grief comes anger and anguish. They look for someone or something to blame. They say things like, 'We have to find the murderer; I'm going to choke him to death,' an angry thirst for revenge. With accidental death they transfer their anger to people like the ambulance driver. They think, 'Maybe there was no one in the hospital emergency room,' or 'Maybe they didn't try long enough.' The parents vent all kinds of irrational hate and anger. We have not only to accept this anger, but help them express it without making them feel guilty."

Preparing for the End

Kübler-Ross says that many patients near death say they wished they had been told they were dying sooner so that they could have prepared themselves and their families.

Other patients approaching death feel a need to cling to a denial of the fact, since the reality of their impending death is too grave a burden to bear. This is fairly rare, however. Of five hundred terminally ill patients dealt with by Kübler-Ross, only four refused to the last to admit that they were dying.

As soon as a dying patient appears willing to talk about the fact of death it is best to help the individual discover what unfinished business needs attention.

When a patient stops denying the certainty of his death there are often feelings of intense anger. The question most often asked is, "Why *me?*" The hostility may be misdirected at hospital staff, friends or family. When the rage over his fate subsides he may begin to bargain with God, in an effort to postpone the inevitable. The question is no longer, "Why *me?*" but "Why *now?*"

With growing acceptance of the inevitability of death, the individual may become depressed, or morose. Some try to make a last minute atonement for wrongs done to family members, or others. Finally, in many instances, the patient begins to mourn his own death. The depression and mourning allow him to become less and less attached to this life and its values, and more adjusted to the approach of death which he now knows to be imminent, or at least inevitable. There are many other variations depending upon the individual's personality, and attitude toward death and immortality.

Making the Most of the Final Days

Very often when people with a terminal illness come to accept the inevitability of their impending death they begin to experience life with a great deal more intensity and appreciation. I think of a friend of mine, suffering with cancer, who spent the last six years of his life knowing that his days were numbered. He told me one day, "I alternate between ecstasy and despair. I am a thousand percent more aware of the beauty around me. I love life profoundly and appreciate it far more than I ever dreamed possible. My emotions are intensely alive. I love more deeply, and care infinitely more about everything. Life has come alive for me. Music sounds more beautiful, and sunsets are unimaginably lovely. But at other times when I dwell on the shortness of the time I have left I go into despair, for I would like to enjoy life—as I now experience it— for another twenty-five or thirty years. But basically, life is richer and better for me than it has ever been."

Kübler-Ross and other thanatologists believe that dying with peace and equanimity need not necessarily be the goal for everyone, since many people were fighters in life, and when the end approaches it finds them still fighting. One of the most important things, many authorities feel, is not to play clever little games with the terminally ill person. "Dishonesty and evasion only add to the guilt and grief and the unfinished business which must be completed before a person can die with dignity. Terminally ill patients, and this includes children as young as four years, know they are not getting well. Often they know more clearly than we in the medical profession *when* they are going to die. They badly need one human being who can listen to them." [6]

One mistake which many friends and relatives often make is to affect a false cheerfulness. "Don't chatter. Admit your turmoil, helplessness and concern. You might say something like, 'I'd like to help but I don't know what to do.' But the most important thing is to listen. Be sensitive to when the dying person wants to talk about what's happening to him. Give him an opening to talk— something like, 'Gee, Dad, it must be hard for you now. Would you like to tell me about it?' Sometimes it is just best to sit and hold his hand." [7]

Asked if she believed in life after death, Kübler-Ross once said in an interview, "I have always felt something significant happens a minute or so after "clinical" death. Most of my patients got fantastically peaceful expressions, even those who had struggled terribly with death." She went on to relate some of her experiences with people who had "died" clinically but had been revived.

Those Who "Died" and Returned

One patient who had been declared dead despite efforts to resuscitate her, came alive three and a half hours later. She told how she had felt, how she had floated out of her physical body and had observed herself lying there, being worked on by the physicians. She described in detail the scene around the operating table, and named the ones who had wanted to abandon the effort, and those who had been determined to continue, and mentioned the one who had told a joke to relieve the tension.

One woman reported on by Kübler-Ross had been "dead" twelve and a half hours. She, along with others who had "come back to life," all related similar impressions and experiences.

Raynor Johnson, an Australian scientist, quotes a man who said, as he approached certain death, "On this occasion I was quite certain (of death) and I remember thinking of things and people I was going to leave. I remember feeling sorry that I hadn't written a masterpiece, that I must leave two people whom I dearly loved, but most of all that I must abandon so many beautiful things, tiny things, the sound of running water, birch trees in the sun, a hot day by the sea, music, reading a good book by the fire, a walk over the hills, and so on. Then with absolute conviction I was aware that I would be leaving nothing; that whatever I had found lovely and of good report I would still enjoy." [8]

Life After Death

Psychiatrist Raymond A. Moody, who holds a doctorate in philosophy as well as a medical degree, became interested in the subject of life after death, and has painstakingly collected and investigated a large number of instances of people "coming back to life" after experiencing clinical death. In a book titled *Life After Life* [9] Dr. Moody describes the amazing similarity of experiences related by the patients who "returned." He says of these patients that "most near-death experiences cannot be readily explained away as delusions induced by pain-killing drugs; the narratives are too clear and too similar to one another." He also asserts that "the picture of the events of dying which emerges from these accounts corresponds in a striking way with that painted in very ancient and esoteric writings totally unfamiliar to my subjects." He found that the experience of floating out of the body, being met by spiritual companions and having an encounter with "a being of light" were remarkably similar to images described in the *Tibetan Book of the Dead*.

The Being Of Light who met all of Dr. Moody's subjects appeared in every instance to be nonjudgmental, but invited the individual to review his or her life; and in what seemed to be but a split second, every detail, large and small, came vividly to the individual's attention. It seemed that the dying person was being asked to judge and evaluate his own life, at a time when rationalizations and evasions were no longer possible, yet there was no accusation or disapproval from the Being of Light.

Psychologist Karlis Osis of the American Society for Psychical Research in New York City has tabulated by computer 877 interviews with physicians who have reported deathbed experiences of this type. In most cases the dying patients saw benign apparitions coming for them. Osis maintains that patients whose brains were impaired by high fever or disease reported fewer visions than those individuals who were fully alert at the time of death.

Proof or Faith?

Such accounts do not "prove" scientifically the survival of the personality after death. Perhaps it is impossible to prove to the satisfaction of everyone the reality of immortality. Jesus said, ". . . Neither will they be convinced if some one should rise from the dead." [10] A considerable number of people witnessed the raising of Lazarus from the dead, and over five hundred persons saw the risen Christ,[11] but this did not constitute proof for those who did not already believe.

Some astute observer noted that "millions of people long for immortality who don't know what to do with themselves on a rainy Sunday afternoon." The hope for, or belief in a continuation of life after death, has resided in the hearts of humans for thousands of years. Cynics would attribute this to a natural distaste for life coming to an end; others believe it is something deeper.

Psychoanalyst Carl Gustav Jung wrote, "If the human soul is anything, it must be of unimaginable complexity and diversity, so that it cannot possibly be approached through a mere psychology of instinct. I can only gaze with wonder and awe at the depths and heights of our psychic nature." [12]

Jung was once asked at a public gathering if he believed in God, and he replied, "I do not believe. . . ." and then paused. One of those present remarked how "the sense of darkness came in the windows of that pause, and how it dissolved swiftly into light when he added, after what seemed an age, 'I *know*.' " [13]

On another occasion Jung said to a friend just before his death, "I can only say that my work has proved empirically that the pattern of God exists in every man and that this pattern has had at its disposal the greatest of all his energies for transformation and transfiguration of his natural being." [14] Jung's last years were spent exploring the relationship between man and the pattern of God in the human spirit.

The great William James of Harvard, father of modern psychology, once remarked in a lecture that "the best argument I know for an immortal life is the existence of a man who deserved one."

There is, at least in the present state of our development, no conceivable way by which immortality can be proven. Jesus did not make any effort to prove it, but far more important, he *demonstrated* it in his death and resurrection. There are probably a number of reasons why some people find it difficult or impossible to believe in immortality.

How Atheists Are Made

I think of a woman whose father, a minister, was almost never at home, since his work as a denominational leader required that he travel a great deal. She assured me dogmatically that "heaven is a myth, just a lot of wishful thinking." After a considerable amount of therapy she came to see the possibility of a connection between an "absentee father," and a "non-existent God." To the small child, Daddy usually represents the supreme authority. This child, always resident within the adult, may feel something like, "Daddy was never there, God is not there, either." Or, in a variation of the same theme, "Daddy was always angry; God is going to be angry with me, too." This connection I have experienced in my own life, and I have observed it in the lives of many others.

Another reason for atheism, the belief that there is no God and hence no heaven, goes something like this in the recesses of the unconscious mind: "Considering the life I have led, if there is a hell I would probably end up there, so I won't believe in hell, or heaven either. If God is the supreme judge, since I don't want to be judged, the best solution is to deny the reality of God, heaven and hell." This all takes place at a deep unconscious level.

A third possible reason has to do with the overintellectualized, schizoid-type personality. These individuals, out of touch with their deep emotions, find satisfaction only in scientific proof, intellectualizations, conceptualizations, theory, and the concomitant insistence on empirical evidence. Many of these people will theorize, and argue, but never seem able to resolve their doubt. Someone put it rather trenchantly, "Never argue with a drunk, an angry woman, or an atheist."

"We die, a few mourn briefly—not so much for us, as for themselves, that they are bereft. The momery fades. Life goes on for them; but what of us? Is there another shore, a spirit-world, where the immortal soul lives on in unimaginable splendor? If so, why is it only hinted at in the Scriptures? Why the secrecy, the mystery, the seeming conspiracy of silence?" [15]

The answer, if there is one, must be that our finite minds are incapable of comprehending, even if we were told, another dimension of time and space, a realm unfathomable to our limited understanding. Jesus said to Nicodemus, "If you disbelieve me when I talk to you about things on earth, how are you to believe if I should talk about the things of heaven?" [16] Perhaps human words are incapable of conveying the mysteries of heaven.

One Who Came Back

Antoinette May, a San Francisco Bay Area journalist who had always been an ardent unbeliever, was a guest at a party given by the artist Walter Keane. Clinging to the edge of the pool she was approached by a drunk who said, "I don't believe you can't swim," and pushed her head under water, holding it there. "It seemed as though hours passed as I tried desperately not to breathe. My lungs were bursting. . . . As I realized that I was dying, my whole life passed before my eyes. This phenomenon is not a novelist's cliche. It *does* occur in the last moments of life. I saw relatives, friends, relived events and conversations.

"Then the parade of past experiences ended and I was suddenly aware of myself hovering ten or twelve feet above the aqua surface of the pool. Though I can hardly make out the big E on an eye chart, I could now see with great clarity. I saw a dark form that was my body under the water, and I could see the man beside me, holding me under the water. . . . At the same time I could hear sounds with equal distinctness, not merely the shrill babble common to any pool party, but separate conversations. I knew exactly what each person was doing and saying.

"The terror of death that had tormented me in the pool was completely gone. Whatever comprised 'I' or 'me,' my personality, would continue, was already continuing. I felt no fear, was totally at ease and luxuriated in being able to breathe comfortably again. . . .

"Then I heard Walter say, 'My God, what are you doing! Let go of her, she'll drown!' I saw him leave his companion and swim toward my body. That's the last thing I remember. . . . In the months and years that followed, I began to probe the unknown. . . . As I researched, interviewed and wrote, I discovered that my own 'out-of-the-body' experience was in no way unique. There are many of us who have died and returned to life." [17]

You and I, my friend, are aging daily, inexorably, and will one day die. If this planet is the grammar school of the universe as some suspect, and if we are to go on growing spiritually and otherwise through unending aeons in another realm, it undoubtedly behooves us not to cut classes, or daydream, but to pay attention to the instructor, to learn well the lessons assigned.

Norman Vincent Peale has expressed it beautifully: "We do not try to prove immortality so that we can believe in it; we try to prove it because we cannot help believing in it. Instinct whispers to us that death is not the end; reason supports it; psychic phenomena uphold it. Even science, in its own way, now insists that the universe is more spiritual than material. Einstein's great equation indicates that matter and energy are interchangeable. Where does that leave us, if not in an immaterial universe? The great psychologist Williams James said: 'Apparently there is one great universal mind, and since man enters into this universal mind he is a fragment of it.' " [18]

One supreme message comes ringing down through the ages from the one they called teacher: "As the Father has loved me, so I have loved you. Dwell in my love. If you heed my commands, you will dwell in my love, as I have heeded my Father's commands and dwell in his love." [19]

8

Self-Esteem and Wholeness

"Through the laughter, dancing, sup-
ping, of people,
Inside of dresses and ornaments, inside
of those wash'd and trimm'd faces,
Behold a secret silent loathing and
despair."

—Walt Whitman

A German couple, back in 1892, worried because their three-year-old boy had not yet learned to say a word. At twenty, the son was a poorly paid office worker, with a side interest in obscure mathematics. The side interest eventually paid off. The son's name was Albert Einstein.

Winston Churchill was deemed a poor student; Napoleon was forty-second in his class; Georg Hegel, the philosopher, was judged by his university as "especially deficient in philosophy." Woodrow Wilson did not do well scholastically in Princeton University, and one of Oliver Goldsmith's teachers described him as the dullest boy she had ever taught.

These were all slow starters. Some psychologists speculate that such late bloomers were troubled as children but managed to achieve a good adjustment later, thus releasing a large part of their potential and skills.

Having a low self-esteem, feeling inferior or inadequate early in life, can be either a powerful stimulus to achievement, or a crushing burden too great to be borne.

An Inferiority Complex Need Not Be Fatal

Harry Stack Sullivan, one of the great psychiatrists of our time, struggled with severe emotional problems and experienced difficulty in relating to people. He had an inadequate education, was casually trained as a physician, but became a great psychiatrist, theorist and teacher, despite an enormous feeling of inferiority. In other

97

words, he suffered from weak self-esteem. One biographer says of him that because of his own emotional problems and extreme diffidence, he was never tempted to stand apart and view his patients as interesting specimens to be studied. He seemed always to see them as suffering individuals, like himself; and the two of them together could learn much, and grow.

Psychologist G. Stanley Hall, a pioneer in his field, once said, "Most of the greatest efforts I ever made in life were to escape inferiority and mediocrity." Most significant achievements have been made by persons who, were they to be asked, would admit that they had experienced feelings of inferiority in some area. And *inferiority* is just another word for low self-esteem or a weak self-image.

Many people with feelings of inadequacy embark on a course of achievement, hoping to win recognition, money, or influence sufficient to dull the inner voice which whispers incessantly, "You're not good enough," or some variation of that judgment. But, as Eric Fromm points out, a person infatuated with money and power tends to act under the illusion that his power and money will increase his self-esteem. Actually they do not serve his real self. He may secure temporary loyalty or friendships or power without bothering to become a likeable or lovable personality; but his insatiable drive for top prizes ultimately alienates people, while he himself is corrupted in the process.

The Three A's—Acceptance, Approval, Affection

Hal was fifty-three-years-old and had achieved his goal of financial success. He came from another state to spend three weeks in daily counseling sessions, seeking to discover the source of his excessive tension and depression. I found him to be rigid and humorless, a man driven by some ancient inner pain to prove that he was a worthwhile person. Now that he had succeeded in business and could afford to retire, he was most unhappy. His mother had given him no affection whatever. An older brother could do no wrong; Hal could do nothing right. Mother was domineering, Dad, passive. In one primal session, after a long silence he heard himself say, with infinite sadness, "I've been lonely all my life." Then, a bit later, "No one likes me, no one accepts me, not even Mom and Dad." Here, then, were the roots of his lack of self-esteem. A fundamental psychological law holds that we tend to get our basic self-image from our parents. If they approve of us and give us the warm love and affirmation we need, we come to think of ourselves as okay persons. If we miss out on the three A's—Acceptance, Approval and Affection—we feel that we are not acceptable. This becomes a deep inner conviction, and no amount of success or affirmation in later life can totally eradicate the feeling, "I don't measure up. I'm not good enough. I'm unacceptable."

How desperately the growing child needs praise, recognition, affirmation. These are aspects of love. A truly loving parent will express approval not only for the child's performance, but for the child himself, as a person. Perhaps once in a hundred years a person may be ruined by excessive praise, but surely once every minute someone dies inside for lack of it.

Jung Healed with Love

A charming incident in the life of Jung is recounted by his biographer, Laurens van der Post. He tells how "a doctor with a practice in a remote mountain district of Switzerland asked Jung to see a simple girl of the hills who, he thought, was going insane. Jung saw her and realized at once that she had neither the intelligence nor the need for a sophisticated and intellectually demanding analytical treatment. . . . Accordingly, he got her to talk to him at length about all the things she had enjoyed and loved as a child. As she talked, almost at once she saw a flicker of interest glow in what had appeared to be burnt-out ashes of herself. He found himself so excited by this quickening of spirit of a despised self that he joined in the singing of her nursery songs and her renderings of her simple mountain ballads. He even danced with her in his library and at times took her on his knee and rocked her in his arms, undeterred by any thoughts of how ridiculous if not preposterous would be the picture of him in the eyes of orthodox medical and psychiatric practitioners when told of what he described with a quiet laugh to me as 'such goings on.'

"At the end of a few days, the girl was fully restored to a state of honor with herself, and he sent her off in high spirits to her home. She never again regressed. Instead . . . the learned doctor in the mountains wrote to Jung and asked him how such results had been achieved. Jung wrote back to the effect, 'I did nothing much. I listened to her fairy tales, danced with her a little, sang with her a little, put her on my knee a little, and the job was done.'" [1]

How little it takes to convey love to a child, and how many millions of children are damaged because parents do not take time to express love and warmth in a form the child can understand. We lecture, admonish, scold, threaten, punish, and scream at them. A typical child may hear twenty criticisms or put-downs for every positive affirmation. The proportion needs to be reversed, if the child is to acquire a proper self-love, and avoid a destructive self-hate.

The Loved Child Has Self-Worth

Lack of self-esteem is not a rare phenomenon, observed only in emotionally damaged personalities. The vast majority of humans suffer from it in some degree, chiefly because of impatient, or hostile, or unloving, unaccepting parents. Jesus deals with the tragic consequences of a weakened sense of self-esteem when he urges his listeners to deal ever so tenderly with small children: "If a man is a cause of stumbling to one of these little ones who have faith in me, it would be better for him to have a millstone hung round his neck and be drowned in the depths of the sea. Alas for the world that such causes of stumbling arise! Come they must, but woe betide the man through whom they come!" [2] The implication is clear: damage done to the tender personality of a child is a sin which is to be judged severely.

The basic, fundamental need of the child, beyond being fed and clothed and sheltered, is to be *loved unconditionally*. If such love is not forthcoming, or if it is given in some distorted form, then the child, grown into an adult, will have an abnormal need to be admired, or noticed, or imitated, or just listened to. The final recourse of the unloved child-become-adult is to go into depression, to become physically or emotionally ill; or if aggressive and violent, filled with rage over not being loved and accepted, such a person may turn to crime.

A television panel dealing with the subject of rape consisted of several women who had been raped and an equal number of men who had been convicted of rape. The men stated that rape was not primarily a sexual attack, but a way of expressing rage over the pain inflicted on them in childhood. Other rapists who have gained insight into their motivation have concurred in the statement that rape is not so much a sexual act as a means of degrading women, whom they have learned to hate because they themselves had felt unloved, degraded and rejected by their mothers.

So the cry goes up: Notice me, listen to me, see that I am alive, a person of worth. Notice me for my performance, or my virtues, or my wealth or achievement. Don't ignore me, for then I feel insignificant, worthless. I want to feel significant, esteemed. Tell me I am a person of worth. But in heaven's name, don't ignore me!

Who Are You?

There is a great confusion existing in the minds of many persons concerning identity. Most people do not know who they are. Ask a dozen people who they are and you will get an interesting variety of responses:

"I am Fred Smith." And the answer, of course, is that Fred Smith is a name but not an identity. Surely he is more than a name.

"I am a wife and mother." Not really. Those are roles and relationships but a role is not an identity.

"I am John P. Brown, a certified public accountant, a Presbyterian, a Mason and a fly fisherman." The name, John Brown, identifies one as distinct from Peter Brown or Bob Fisher, but is not an identity; and being a CPA is a vocation; Presbyterian is a denomination, the Masons are a secret society, and fly fishing is a sport. None of these has to do with his identity.

I possess a body, but I am not my body. My body may be healthy or sick, tired or rested. That has nothing to do with the real "I." I have emotions, but I am not my emotions. They are constantly changing, never the same, but I remain myself. I may feel anger, love, despair, exaltation, awe, reverence, jealousy, or many other emotions, but the "I" within remains the same, whether I experience joy or sorrow, whether I am excited or calm, at worship or at work.

Since I observe and am aware of my emotions it is obvious that I am separate and distinct from them, for I experience them, control and direct them.

I have an intellect, but I am not my intellect. It accumulates knowledge, facts, and thousands of bits of random information, but it is not myself. I possess this intellect, but it is not me.

I am a center of conscious awareness. I am conscious that I am aware, as no animal can be. I am aware of myself as a rational-emotional being. This consciousness which is the core of "me" is capable of directing and utilizing all of my physical, intellectual, emotional and spiritual processes. I direct these processes. This center of pure consciousness is made in the image of God. It is spirit, created from the same essence of which God consists. It is, in short, god.

This inner god-self, the "I," is spelled with a small *g*, for I am not God, but a god. Jesus affirms this: "You are gods." [3] He had been accused of blasphemy for equating himself with God. In reply he quoted from Psalm 82. For some reason this is a text that is seldom if ever quoted. Most Christians are not aware that Jesus made this statement. It is studiously avoided in our Bible study and preaching. It is too threatening. But there it is, in both the Old and New Testaments: "You are gods." You, then, are a god encapsulated in a physical body. That is your true identity.

What Is Your Identity?

I recall a man who had been a great success as a rancher. Some years after reaching retirement age he sold his ranch and decided to take it easy. Unfortunately, he had made no plans for retirement. A person should really make definite plans for the retirement years, starting ten years ahead of the event.

But my friend didn't have time to plan that far ahead. Having no hobbies and no interest to occupy his mind, he became morose, then depressed. Physicians gave him the usual anti-depressants, which are fine for temporary use, but cure nothing. He lived quite some distance away, and I was unaware of his deepening depression. Finally, one day he rigged up a shot gun to a post and pulled the trigger, thus ending his terribly unhappy life.

He was a fine Christian man, but a depression that deep, I am told by persons who have weathered it, is indescribably terrible. It amounts to temporary insanity. The suicidal man had no real identity apart from "rancher." He had spent his life seeing himself as a rancher, and without that false role-identity he was nothing. Many persons who do not commit suicide suddenly, do so gradually and die prematurely, if they do not have a genuine sense of identity.

In a world of distorted values a person can devalue himself because he has not accumulated as much of this world's goods as his neighbor, or is not as "successful." By comparing oneself to high achievers and the more advantaged, one can come to feel inferior. This minimizes one's self-esteem. A person may be led to devalue himself because he drives a twelve-year-old car, lives on the wrong side of the tracks, or because he was a C student and didn't finish college. Granted that some of this low opinion may be founded on what other people think, let's face the fact that most feelings of inferiority are based on what we think of ourselves.

A Self-accepting Church Custodian

I often think with pleasure of Joe, for over twenty-five years the custodian of the church where I once served. He came over as a refugee after World War II, with his wife and small son. Speaking no English, he was put to work temporarily as janitor until an English-speaking one could be found. But he remained because he became so absolutely indispensable. He learned not only to speak English, he also learned plumbing, carpentry, electrical work, gardening and a host of other things. Joe may have reached only the seventh grade in the Ukraine where he was reared, but it never crossed his mind to think that he was less important than the Americans who drove Cadillacs. On Wednesday evening he would go home and change clothes. All dressed up he would reappear at the social hall to greet people attending the Family Night Dinner. I am sure that he was more loved than I, and I rejoiced in it because he is a lovable person who accepts himself. He has humility with self-esteem. He loves people and they love him, not only because he is the world's greatest custodian, but because he is a warm, loving person. It would never cross his mind to think of himself as unloved or unappreciated.

Incidentally, his cleverness did not extend only to the church buildings. He knew how to handle money. On a slender income he saved and invested so well that after twenty-five years in this country he owns an apartment building now worth over half a million dollars, plus other property. Half the church membership would like to know how he did it.

My point is this: If you lack self-esteem, it is not because you do not have enough education, or money, or because you are not physically attractive. It is solely because of your own evaluation of yourself. And this has come about largely because of your early childhood. It is not your fault.

We get our basic sense of self-worth from parents and other authority figures. If you did not get enough affirmation and love to make you feel worthwhile or okay, then you can begin to work on your weak self-image.

I listened for two hours to a man whom I had regressed to childhood in a Primal Integration session. Feeling about three or four years old, he reexperienced intensely events and feelings of that age and began to say in a little boy's voice, "I'm not good enough. I'm no good. I'm a bad boy. Mommy doesn't love me. I'm just no good. Mommy, please love me; Mommy, Mommy, Mommy!" Then followed tears and pleadings that lasted for the better part of two hours. He does not blame his mother, whom he feels did her best. He knows that she was damaged by her parents; but in reliving the primal hurts he was discharging the encapsulated hurts of infancy and childhood. He spent many hours reliving those childhood experiences and emotions before he gained a genuine sense of worth.

Thousands of hours of experience in this type of therapy have demonstrated that the discharging of these feelings liberates psychic energy which has been used to hold those repressed feelings out of consciousness. People who have been damaged by childhood hurts or by the deprivation of love end up with a better self-image after reliving those traumatic childhood events.

Ancient Hurts Must Be Discharged

The child accepts unquestioningly the verbal or unspoken evaluation. The child, who may be loved but who for some reason *feels* unloved, grows up with low self-esteem. He can become whole when he has dealt therapeutically with the ancient hurts which have deprived him of his self-worth.

A minister, having relived some of his own childhood hurts in a primal session, said, "I have been preaching a very simplistic gospel, assuring people that when they placed all their burdens at the foot of the cross, they would be totally new creatures in Christ, with all anxieties banished and most of their problems solved. That's a bunch of rubbish! I now realize that one act of repentance and a single commitment does not necessarily rid one of the accumulated emotional and spiritual debris of a lifetime. How I wish it did! I see now that after three years with Jesus, Simon Peter was still a mixed-up person. Most of the rest of the Twelve were, too. Even living and working with him, and seeing him as the Son of God, did not rid them instantly or magically of their emotional hangups." There was a pause. Then, "Tomorrow, let's go down again and get another load of those hurts and dump them. I would have told you that I had a pretty good childhood, and I guess I did; but even so, I got damaged and my self-image suffered." And we did. In subsequent hours he became much more a whole person, after reliving innumerable hurts of the past.

A strong self-image, high self-esteem, a strong ego—these terms have nothing to do with egotism. Let's define our terms:

A Big Ego Is Desirable

Ego means basically the *self*. Psychoanalytically it also has other meanings.

Egotism means an exaggerated sense of self-importance. It nearly always springs from a feeling of inferiority. It is an effort to compensate for weak self-esteem. The braggart, the name-dropper, the person who talks too much about himself or herself does not have a "big ego" but a little one; that is, a low self-worth.

Ego-centric refers to the trait of being extremely self-centered, which may be with or without egotism. The ego-centric person is usually partially or totally oblivious of the needs or interests or feelings of other people.

What we need is not a small ego, but a larger, healthier one. A large ego means a large degree of self-acceptance. One with a weak ego is either shy and withdrawn, with feelings of inferiority, or loud and aggressive and possibly argumentative and opinionated. A passive person with low self-esteem will tend to be withdrawn, while the aggressive self-hater will project his aggression onto others in the form of hostility, domination, or just plain offensive conduct.

We Have a Right to Love Ourselves

Dr. Hans Selye says, "The fact remains that we have a right to love ourselves properly, and to be concerned with ourselves. If I do not give primary concern to my own interests, it is not likely that anyone else is going to do so." [4] Jesus urges us to have a three-fold love experience with God, our neighbor and ourself.

For one to be overly-compliant, excessively devoted to the welfare of another, and to ignore his or her own interests would appear to be rather neurotic. This in no way deprecates the self-sacrifice of a missionary who immerses himself or herself in some primitive culture in order to minister to them. This is not a neurotic altruism, but simply doing what gives the greatest degree of satisfaction.

This type of dedication is far removed from the overly-compliant, neurotic, self-sacrificing act of a young woman I knew. She was talented, very attractive, and had many boyfriends. Her father, however, strongly disapproved of every young man she dated. When the young woman's mother died the father became even more protective and determined to keep his daughter at home by various strategems. At age sixty she was still unmarried, having refused half-a-dozen proposals at her father's insistence. She was sixty-seven when she buried her father. Her face bore the patient, resigned look of a self-sacrificing daughter who had permitted life to pass her by. Her selfish ego-centric father had been more concerned about his own welfare than that of his daughter. By keeping her at home he had a free housekeeper who was self-supporting, and a combination wife-mother-daughter and nurse in his old age. His daughter, made overly-compliant and passive, lived a largely unfulfilled life due to her weak self-esteem.

The Struggle for Self-Esteem

The struggle for self-esteem begins early in childhood, from the first day of life. It reveals itself very profoundly in sibling rivalry. Ernest Becker writes, "In childhood we see the struggle for self-esteem at its least disguised. The child is unashamed about what he needs and wants most. His whole organism shouts the claims of his natural narcissism. And this claim can make childhood hellish for the adults concerned, especially when there are several children competing at once for the prerogatives of limitless self-extension. . . . We like to speak casually about 'sibling rivalry' as though it were some kind of by-product of growing up, a bit of competitiveness and selfishness of children who have been spoiled, who haven't yet grown into a generous social nature. . . . The child

cannot allow himself to be second best or devalued, much less left
out. 'You gave him the biggest piece of candy.' 'You gave him
more juice.' 'Here's a little more then.' 'Now she's got more juice
than me.' 'You let her light the fire in the fireplace and not me.'
'Okay, you light a piece of paper.' 'But this piece of paper is
smaller than the one she lit.' . . . and so on. It is not that children
are vicious, selfish, or domineering. It is that they so openly express
man's tragic destiny: he must desperately justify himself as an object
of primary value in the universe; he must stand out, be a hero,
and make the biggest possible contribution to world life, show that
he *counts* more than anything or anyone else." [5]

The need to feel important, or at least significant, is universal.
Sometimes this drive can be destructive. "Half the harm that is
done in this world," says the psychiatrist in T.S. Eliot's *The Cocktail Party,*

> Is due to people who want to feel important.
> They don't mean to do harm—but the harm does not
>   interest them.
> Or they do not see it, or they justify it
> Because they are absorbed in the endless struggle
> To think well of themselves.[6]

To Be Unloved Is to Be Depressed

Montaigne once said that of all the infirmities we have, the
most savage is to despise our being. I saw this truth epitomized in
a rather depressed middleaged woman who, as I learned in extensive counseling sessions with her, had never known love as a child.
The daughter of wealthy, sophisticated, unfeeling and unloving
parents, she wept herself to sleep every night for lack of being
touched and held. Around the age of eleven she learned the magic
power of turning off feelings so she wouldn't hurt. She became a
totally non-feeling person. Her voice was a flat monotone tinged
with an all-pervasive sadness. She never became angry, never felt
love, nor any other emotion for that matter. She married, but felt
guilty over feeling nothing and giving nothing to her husband.
In some Primal Integration sessions she relived her tragic childhood.
At first the sessions consisted of nothing but violent choking,
heart-breaking sobs which she tried unsuccessfully to stifle. "I never
cry," she said apologetically. "I hate to cry." But cry she did, hour
after hour as she relived her pain-filled childhood.

One aspect of her personality which interested me was that she
denigrated herself. Compliments, which she desperately needed
and wanted, were turned aside with a deprecating response. She
could see no virtue in herself, no strength, no value. She was almost

entirely without self-esteem. Only as she allowed herself to re-experience her painful childhood did she acquire some self-worth and begin to see herself as basically a delightful person, capable of great warmth and depth of feeling.

Fritz Perls conceived of the neurotic structure as consisting of four layers. The first two involve role playing, cliches, small talk, glib empty phrases—the means and methods almost everyone uses to "get along" in polite society. The vast majority of people live out their lives on these first two layers. The third layer is difficult to penetrate. This one covers our feelings, our fear, loneliness, inferiority, and often our tenderness and love. This is the level which we try to conceal or deny with our defense systems and rationalizations. We feel that to be known at this level could make us vulnerable or be embarrassing. "One doesn't show such feelings to the world." The fourth layer, the most baffling in a sense, is the almost totally denied feeling of terror, the fear of death, the sense of panic originating in childhood, feelings of abandonment, help-lessness and utter dependency. As we peel back the top layers and get down to the underlying primal fears and hurts we can become truly authentic persons.

The Road to a Better Self-Image

The sad and disquieting news is that it is not easy to build a better self-image. There is no magic formula. But the good news is that it can be done, in time. The truth has been tucked away in an old and much misunderstood book—the Bible.

Most people associate the Bible with religion, devotions, church services, and morality, sometimes with grim prohibitions, and dire warnings of an angry God. The fact of the matter is that Jesus said little or nothing about religion, but a vast deal about life and how to live it.

For instance, he gave some deathless principles which many read as devotional material and then feel a little better momentarily; but the Sermon on the Mount [7] was never intended to be used as inspirational material. It is to be applied—and not for God's sake, but for our own.

Here are two simple principles from the Sermon on the Mount which, if practiced, would improve anyone's self-image:

1. "Give and it shall be given unto you." [8]
2. "Love your enemies, and pray for those who persecute you. If you love those who love you, what reward have you?" [9]

There is a vast deal more in that Magna Carta of the Soul, *The Sermon on the Mount*. But just take those two principles as a starting point, and let's see what they would imply:

Give! Instead of waiting for life to give to you, start giving!

Don't wait for others to introduce themselves; introduce *yourself.*
Give friendliness, warmth, and show interest in the other person.
If you don't feel it, it's because you haven't practiced it, and it's
buried beneath your loneliness and hurt.

Give compliments. No one was ever offended by a sincere compliment. If you feel insincere, again, it is from lack of practice.
Plautus said, "I much prefer a compliment, even if insincere, to
sincere criticism." Notice what people are wearing, doing, thinking,
planning. Manifest an interest in the other person. Turn the spot-
light on the other individual instead of waiting for attention to be
focused on you. Give, Jesus said, and it will be given to you. Life
returns to the giver much more than to the taker. If you don't
feel like it, do it anyway! Jesus never told people what to feel, only
what to do. This doesn't mean that feelings are unimportant, only
that in many instances feelings follow actions, as William James
demonstrated long ago.

Love. Give love in whatever form seems appropriate. A compliment is one facet of love, but there are many more. When you
show genuine interest in another person, you are manifesting
agape-love. When you offer to help another person or respond
with a *yes* to human need, you are giving love. For love is not just
an emotion; it is also an action.

A woman told me the tragic story of her divorce after sixteen
years of marriage. That was devastating enough, but even worse,
all four of her children chose to live with the father. I felt her
deep hurt and sense of abandonment, but it was not difficult to
understand the reason for her having been abandoned. She had so
little self-esteem that she spent virtually every waking hour in an
effort to *get* love and appreciation from others. She was a depressed, self-rejecting, complaining martyr whose self-pity and
criticism would cause even the most charitable to avoid her. My
appraisal of her personality is not a criticism but an objective fact.
I recognized that her childhood had marred her, and for that she
was not responsible; but she was responsible for making some
changes in her self-defeating attitudes. We can give her credit for
seeking counseling so that she could get to the root of her problem.

Instead of complaining, and waiting, and hoping for life to
happen to you, you must happen to life. Give! If you don't know
where to start, then back up one step and "Ask . . . seek . . .
knock. . . . " [10] That is, batter down some doors, ask where help
can be found, and keep at it until you find some answers. Let
nothing defeat you.

Instead of wondering why you are not invited out more, try
doing the inviting. If you get some negative responses, keep at it!

If you keep on getting what you feel is rejection, ask some objective, qualified persons if there is something about you that causes you to be rejected.

Begin Now Where You Are

Instead of trying to build your self-esteem quickly by achieving something of great significance, build by degrees. Start wherever you can and do the best possible job. Let your performance speak for you. Avoid criticism and negative reactions, and if there are people around you who enjoy gossip and character assassination, avoid them at all costs. Negativism is self-defeating.

If you are hurting, as millions are, you naturally want some quick results. Everyone does. All of us are impatient in some degree. But the biggest rewards go to those who take the long-range view, and exercise love, joy, peace, patience, kindness, goodness, fidelity, gentleness, and self-control.[11] These nine virtues are called "the harvest of the spirit" by the Apostle Paul. If you cannot manifest all those qualities at once—and who can all the time!—practice the ones within your reach. A harvest is not reaped without effort. Before the harvest there is plowing, harrowing, cultivating, planting, irrigating or waiting for rain, and *then* the harvest—which in itself is hard work.

Those nine strengths or virtues are called "fruits of the spirit" in some translations, which could suggest lucious fruit hanging there on the tree just waiting to be plucked and eaten. I much prefer the more realistic New English Bible translation, which calls this "the harvest of the spirit," because to get a harvest, you must work; and work is an integral part of life.

Begin, my friend, if you want earnestly to have a better self-image, if you desire to like yourself, to love yourself properly. There is a saying: "They also serve who only stand and wait." It would be more apt to say, "They also *starve* who only stand and wait"; starve, that is, for the good things of life. Get in motion! And let nothing stop you.

9

Guilt and Wholeness

"We only acknowledge small faults in order to make it appear that we are free from great ones."
—La Rochefoucauld

Let's face it, you and I are guilty. I don't know the details of your guilt, nor do you know mine. But guilty we are, for it is a universal condition. Everyone is guilty. I share with you the burden of knowing that "all alike have sinned, and are deprived of the divine splendour. . . . " [1] Let's look at the facts, and then see what we can do about the situation.

Employees steal more than $10 million a *day* in cash and merchandise—about $3 billion a year, according to Norman Jaspen, president of a firm with forty years experience in the detection and prevention of white-collar crime. He has discovered that this dishonesty spreads from the executive suite to the warehouse dock, and includes sales clerks and office workers. Most inside crimes are committed by trusted employees. One in ten employees is a thief. Whether our guilt consists of overt acts of dishonesty, or the more socially acceptable sins of the spirit—pride, envy, greed, lust—we are all tarred with the same brush and marred by our own particular form of evil.

Time Does Not Diminish Guilt

One aspect of guilt not generally understood is that time does not diminish guilt in the slightest. The emotional-spiritual self has no awareness of past, present or future. Unresolved guilt goes on doing its damage to the personality year after year.

A minister serving a large church told me that twenty years earlier he had stolen thirty-five cents from the cash register of a place where he worked part time. He felt an urgent need to go back and make restitution, since, as he said, "It isn't the amount of

110

money involved, it's my dishonesty that has begun to bother me." He found the firm had gone out of business and felt a need to share his boyhood guilt with me in order to gain a sense of freedom from his accusatory conscience.

Unfortunately, we often confess some lesser sin to avoid facing up to an unacknowledged larger sin we would rather not face. These things are dealt with therapeutically in Primal Integration sessions. A woman undergoing this type of therapy shared what she called "the dark secrets of my past," which I felt probably concealed some more basic problem. In a primal session she relived important forgotten scenes from her rigid fundamentalist background and came to see that the judgmental preaching had left her with a warped, overly-sensitive conscience, condemning her for things for which she had felt needlessly guilty for years. She finally went into a rage, beautiful in its intensity and honesty, over the way authoritarian parents and legalistic preachers had damaged her personality. Finally exhausted, she said, "I don't blame them. They did their sorry best, but it's great to know how it all started and that I'm not all that bad a person."

Self-Hate and Physical Health

In any deep long-standing depression there is often a component of self-hate, a sense of loss, and guilt, real or false. Usually there is some form of malnutrition regardless of how good one's diet may be or how many vitamins the person may be taking. In a therapy group Jean, a divorcee in her forties, exhibited both depression and violent anger. A year with a therapy group produced insight but little benefit. I suggested that she get checked out for hypoglycemia and thyroid imbalance. Tests revealed that she did indeed have hypoglycemia (low blood sugar), and she went on a proper diet. Improvement, however, was slight, and I knew there was more to look into. I suggested a mineral test, which revealed a severe imbalance, especially high copper and low zinc, which often predisposes one toward erratic behavior and emotional distress.

When her mineral imbalance was rectified over a period of several months, there was some slight improvement, but not enough. She was still depressed and angry. In some primal sessions she began to uncover ancient childhood hurts—the loss of her father, rejection and ridicule by her family, and numerous other childhood traumas. Eventually she got into a scene, long buried in her unconscious, in which she was being raped. Her repressed fear and rage were expressed and discharged in a number of violent episodes. Now the change in her personality was fantastic. Her rage toward her children, mixed with loving concern, gave way to more understanding and patience. Her harsh, angry approach to life diminished, and she became far more gentle and loving.

Her fear, rage, guilt and inferiority had all merged into a single, nameless emotion which distorted her personality and destroyed her relationships. Hers had been an emotional, spiritual, physical and relational problem. No simplistic solution could have resolved it.

All One Emotion

Feelings of inferiority, shame, guilt, poverty and failure all seem to register on the emotional structure as the same basic emotion. It is almost impossible to distinguish between them. I was once visiting the most primitive Indian tribe on the North American continent, the Tarahumaras. It's a long train ride from Chihuahua, Mexico, to the little mining town of Creel. From there one takes a jeep over rough roads to an extremely wild and inaccessible part of Mexico where the timid, gentle Tarahumaras live, scattered through the mountains. There is a school and tiny church at the small settlement.

One morning, observing the tattered rags being worn by some of the boys lined up outside the school I began to take pictures, thinking that a graphic portrayal of their extreme poverty would help me raise money for new clothes back home—as indeed it did. But as I looked through the view finder of my camera I observed two wretchedly dressed boys cringing in adject shame, trying fruitlessly to conceal their filthy rags which were virtually falling off of them. I almost wept as I saw how horribly ashamed they were of their terrible poverty. They couldn't know my motives, and there was no way I could explain. The expression on their faces and the cringing postures they assumed were identical with those of a person experiencing intense guilt and shame. Sigmund Freud has pointed out that it is virtually impossible to distinguish between inferiority feelings and guilt. I saw this graphically demonstrated in the picture of those pathetic boys, which helped me raise enough money to clothe every child in the school.

The Self-punishing Personality

What unresolved guilt does to us is illustrated by an account of one of Carl Gustav Jung's patients. As related by Jung's biographer, Laurens van der Post:

"She arrived at his office one morning, refused to give her name, and was to walk out of both the office and Jung's life without revealing it. . . . She had admitted only that she was a doctor and went on to confess that years ago she had killed her best friend in order to marry her husband. The murder was never discovered and in due course she married the man and had a daughter by him. Consciously, she had no moral compunction over what she had done. . . .

"Such unease as there was appears to have been felt by nature, and the atmosphere of murder communicated itself to all around her, through the damage it had done to her own inner personality. First, her husband died soon after the marriage. The daughter grew up estranged from her and ultimately vanished without trace from her life. Her friends one after the other abandoned her; soon even the animals whom she loved appeared afraid of her. For instance, she loved riding but had to give it up because the horses she had hitherto managed so well became nervous of her and shied; ultimately she was thrown by one of her favorite mounts. She was left only with her dogs and clung to them. Then her favorite dog, too, had to be destroyed and she could bear the exile from life and nature no longer. She came to Jung to confess, and after confession left, and he was to see and hear from her no more. . . . Jung commented, 'Sometimes it seems as if even animals and plants know [about our guilt].' " [2]

There is often a close relationship between guilt and illness. In speaking of unconscious guilt, that is, guilt of which the individual is unaware but still feels unconsciously, Freud wrote, "The patient must not be healthy, he must remain ill, for he (feels he) deserves no better. . . . The sense of guilt also offers an explanation of the cure or improvement of severe neurosis. . . . It does not tell him he is guilty; he does not feel guilty, he simply feels ill. This sense of guilt expresses itself only as resistance to recovery which is extremely difficult to overcome." [3]

Self-induced Failure

We have already seen how failure, guilt, inferiority, and shame register as the same emotion. I recall a friend who felt all of those emotions but could not admit any one of them to consciousness, though they were quite obvious even to a casual observer. He was a young minister whose education was rather limited, and who had an impoverished childhood. Thus, he felt inferior. He had not succeeded well in his first church and felt a sense of failure. He experienced shame and guilt over the fact that he could relieve his enormous anxiety and tension only by drinking, often to excess.

He suffered a series of illnesses which required hospitalization. There were a number of accidents for which he did not seem directly to blame. He did not succeed in a major expansion program, and this registered as failure. So, without being at all aware of the raging forces within, but feeling failure, guilt, shame and rejection, he became seriously ill and was hospitalized. Upon release, he became emotionally ill and began to drink heavily, all the while blaming others for his disasters. Eventually he became an alcoholic and was again hospitalized, then released. He disappeared, and his family was forced to look elsewhere for support.

Most of our punishment for real or false guilt is not so devastating. I have found myself coming down with a severe cold, sometimes leading to "flu," as the result of emotions about which I felt vaguely guilty but unable to resolve soon enough to ward off physical illness. It was only by looking back that I could see the pattern.

Very often people confess to the wrong sin, fault or crime, in an unconscious effort to secure release. Valerie Percy, twenty-one-year-old daughter of Senator Charles H. Percy, was murdered in her home in September 1966. Illinois police conducted more than ten thousand interviews and followed up more than thirteen hundred tips, without avail. There were *nineteen false confessions* to the murder. There were sixty false confessions to a murder committed in Miami, Florida. Over a hundred fake confessions were made to a Chicago murder. When there is a serious crime which generates a vast amount of newspaper publicity a large number of people, innocent of that particular crime, will confess, apparently in an effort to resolve guilt over other crimes or guilt feelings, and sometimes in the pathetic need to secure a certain amount of notoriety. People whose lives are drab and uneventful, and who feel a great need for love, willingly substitute notoriety for love which is not available. It goes like this: love me, notice me; if you won't see me as a person of worth, at least notice me, if not as having worth, then because I have done something, anything, to merit attention. I will take negative attention, even blame, if you will only pay me some attention.

Shared Guilt

There is such a thing as corporate or shared guilt. A case in point is that of a severely distressed young married woman who came to me for counseling. Sensing that she needed temporary medication I sent her to a physician who prescribed a tranquillizer and anti-depressant. He phoned to discuss the case, and we agreed that she needed supportive friends. I conferred with an associate and asked him to see that she was integrated into a social group, and then phoned a sister and brother-in-law to urge them to offer emotional support. I asked the young woman to return for further counseling.

A week later she committed suicide. All of us who were involved in her life felt devastated. At the funeral service, which I conducted, I said, "I am certain that all of us here feel a sense of both individual and corporate guilt. In one sense we are all jointly guilty, for none of us did enough. Had we only known that she would try to take her life, each of us would have made far more of an effort. But we were busy, wrapped up in our own interests. We can never know fully the mind of another person. None of us followed through adequately, and each of us is in some degree guilty. I am not trying to make you feel guilty; I am only pointing out what is true so that in the future when there is a call for help, we will respond with adequate love and support."

"All Have Sinned. . . . "

It is not a cop-out to remind ourselves that all of us, without exception, suffer from some degree of moral or spiritual rot. The Apostle Paul writes, "I know I am rotten through and through so far as my old sinful nature is concerned. . . . " [4] The Bible says, " . . . David is a man after my own heart, for he will obey me. . . . " [5] Yet David experienced at least one great moral lapse, involving the death of a man and the seduction of his wife. Solomon, described in the Bible as the wisest man who had ever lived, gave evidence in his later years of moral and spiritual decadence. The outer trappings of his kingdom showed every sign of opulence, grandeur and power, but his leadership was so weak and unwise in the final years of his reign that the kingdom collapsed immediately after his death.

The twelve Apostles were spiritually and intellectually confused, and lacked even the most rudimentary understanding of what Jesus was trying to teach them. Like them, we are each a mixture of truth and error, weakness and strength, greed and unselfishness, and a host of other moral and spiritual ambivalences.

One man, all too aware of the human predilection for failure and weakness, has a card standing on his desk which reads:

> There is something wrong with you—
> And with me.
> If you will overlook my weaknesses and mistakes
> I will be glad to overlook yours.

Substitutes for Personal Morality

I liked Joe personally. He was physically attractive, highly intelligent, though rather unsure of his masculinity. He was a member of a therapy group I conducted and seemed to be succeeding

rather well in his ministry. He was trying to decide whether or not
to divorce his wife, with whom he had little in common, and marry
a member of the church with whom he was falling in love. He felt
vaguely guilty over the situation, but strangely enough expressed
no particular sense of guilt over having had sexual relations with
two women in his congregation. After sharing that bit of information, he began to complain rather bitterly over the fact that he
couldn't get the members of his congregation aroused over tragic
world conditions.

The group digested this for a few moments, then one of the
members asked, gently, and non-judgmentally, "Joe, is your zeal
for social justice a substitute for personal morality?" He looked
startled. After a moment's silence he said, "Yes, that's possible. I
want to think about it." Joe didn't like having to face this, and
he soon dropped the group.

One cannot be whole who will not be honest. Honesty with
oneself, with others, and with God, is the first all-important step
toward spiritual growth and wholeness.

What is right, and what is wrong? It is not always spelled out
specifically in the Bible. To some degree morality is whatever the
majority agree upon in a given culture, at any particular time,
with the exception of such fundamental moral principles as are
taught in the Ten Commandments and the Sermon on the Mount.

Even the interpretation of these biblical commandments may
differ with changing times. I can recall a time when women on
the beach of Lake Michigan, in Chicago, were arrested and taken
to jail for not wearing stockings with their bathing suits. I can
remember angry and fiery sermons preached in my boyhood on the
evils of women wearing "bobbed" hair. Scriptures were quoted to
validate the charge that it was evil.

We have an interesting way of changing our values and standards to suit our needs. All agree that it is wrong to kill; yet in
time of war men are decorated and acclaimed as heroes for mass
killings. The men who dropped the atom bomb on Hiroshima,
killing an estimated 85,000 people, were decorated. An even larger
number of people were killed in the mass bombings of Germany
during World War II, when entire cities were reduced to rubble.

How Conscience Develops

Conscience is not always an infallible guide. When we come into
the world as infants we do not have a conscience on which are
inscribed the Ten Commandments, the teachings of Jesus, and
the vehicle code, together with a list of the social niceties. Right
is taught by parents and other authority figures: it is wrong to

kill, except in time of war; it is wrong to hit your playmates except in self-defense; don't talk with your mouth full; don't tell dirty stories, and ten thousand other prohibitions and exhortations.

Obeying the Higher Law

The enlightened conscience, growing in sensitivity to the will of God, can finally be liberated from the law and become subject to the higher principle of love for God, others, and self. Wholeness involves the ability to transcend man-made laws with the higher law of love where the two conflict. Some conscientious objectors base their refusal to serve in the armed forces upon a law which they deem to be higher than the laws of the nation. Jesus violated the law, in the eyes of the priests, on more than one occasion. He ate with unwashed hands, did a work of healing on the Sabbath, and husked grain on the Sabbath in violation of current laws.

What, then, is sin at its core? One might compile half a hundred definitions. Here is one which seems to satisfy me, based as it is on the Law of Love: Sin is anything I do, or fail to do, which harms another person; it is anything which I do, or fail to do, which harms me. Sin is failing to do, within my power, what I can to help another. Sin is failure to live in love with God and man.

Confess the Faulty Self, Not the Symptom

I ceased long ago to confess merely the act. The act, or failure to act appropriately, is only symptomatic of an impaired, faulty self. When I experience a feeling of guilt, I sense that this is a warning bell, urging me to reexamine my actions or my inner self. After reviewing the guilty act, I then go back to the faulty self in which the act originated. If I am suddenly and unreasonably angry and dump my anger on another, I do not confess this guilty act; I confess the guilty *self* and try to discover what prompted me to act inappropriately. If I search long enough I may find that behind my anger is fear, as it is so often the case. So, now I can acknowledge fear, the basic emotion, and can say, "Lord, I got unreasonably angry at someone. I'm sorry it happened, but there is something deeper, my fear—fear of losing an argument, fear of loss of face, fear of being controlled or manipulated. I now confess this impaired, fearful self. I'll probably remain this way unless you help me." Having examined the sin and its roots, and having confessed it, I am now free to say, "God accepts and forgives me, and so I will now forgive and accept myself." At this point, whether the self-examination takes ten minutes or two days, I need to drop the whole matter. There is no point in self-condemnation once we are forgiven by God and self.

"Guilty" of Not Having Been Loved

In a series of counseling sessions a middle-aged man, riddled with generalized guilt feelings originating in his childhood, talking to himself, to God and me, said, vehemently, "I see that I am not all that guilty. I am guilty of not having been loved, if that is guilt at all. Now as a result I can't love anyone. I feel like telling my pastor, 'You tell me every Sunday that I am a sinner and how bad I am. I'm not going to pay you any more to tell me I'm bad. I *know* I'm bad, or at least I feel that way. I don't want to keep on hearing it. I need to be *loved!*' "

Many of our intellectualizations and philosophical rationalizations are an effort to avoid facing real guilt. Unfortunately, the spiritual-emotional self does not accept rationalizations. I recall a woman who at one time belonged to a Yokefellow group which I led. She rejoiced over the fact that she was a non-practicing alcoholic and sought still greater growth. One day she came to my office to tell me that she was leaving the church because she could no longer believe in the divinity of Jesus. She was not argumentative, just firm. A year or so later I discovered the reason. Just before leaving the church she and her husband had been on an ocean cruise, and though she knew alcoholics should never drink again, she weakened and began to drink socially. This worked all right for six months or so, then she discovered to her horror that she was once again a practicing alcoholic. Attendance at AA meetings did not resolve the problem this time. She went to a rehabilitation center for alcoholics, where she spent six months "drying out." Her declaration that she could no longer believe the Bible was the rationalization for her determination to try drinking again. Thus do our subtle rationalizations betray us.

It is very difficult for one to want a close relationship with God at the same time he is determined upon a course he knows to be out of harmony with the will of God. Such a one hides behind rationalizing verbiage as Adam once hid from God behind the foliage.

Mistakes, Sins, Failures

I find it difficult to distinguish the feelings I experience when I make a mistake, commit a sin, fail in some enterprise, or simply discover that I have been guilty of an overreaction. I am embarrassed when I wake in the middle of the night (when, in the darkness, every defect is magnified) and think of all my inappropriate actions, responses and overreactions. I never need to look farther than yesterday to find some evidence of immaturity or some lack of wholeness. I can always discover times when I was over-sensitive, evidenced pride or defensiveness, experienced the emotions of greed or impatience, or bore some silly little grudge. I think of all the times—clear back to childhood if the night is very dark—when I blew it, and for a few moments I wallow in remorse and guilt. Now there are several alternatives:

1. I can push this out of my mind, in the realization that I am only human and must not dwell on such negative things. Unfortunately, thoughts pushed out of the conscious mind go into the unconscious where they carry on their nefarious work.

2. I can justify my actions, rationalize them, and marshall a score of reasons for my defects, but they don't convince my emotions.

3. I can focus on these malfunctioning aspects of my personality and become morbidly depressed; for anger at the self invariably produces depression.

4. Or, I can examine those areas of immaturity (another name for unwholeness), thank God that all or most of them can be learning experiences, and be glad I can profit from them. I can now confess to God not the overt act, or failure, but the impaired self. Aware that divine forgiveness does not always provide a sense of cleansing (else why do we go on confessing the same sin over and over?), I can proceed to forgive myself, much as I would forgive another person. Being disposed to self-condemnation—a product of my fundamentalist childhood—I will need to affirm this self-forgiveness numerous times until I genuinely feel it.

A saint has been defined as one who confesses more and more and sins less and less. With this thought in mind I am not losing ground just because I confess more often and with deeper feelings of remorse.

Conversion of a Murderer

Susan Atkins, after one of the longest trials in California history, was sentenced to death for her part in the 1969 Charles Manson "Tate murders." On Death Row, Susan began to read the Bible and, as a result, became a professing Christian in her little cell. She shared this with the prison chaplain, along with her fear that her new-found faith would be misconstrued on the outside, and asked that it be kept as quiet as possible.

Susan requested baptism by immersion. Since there were no facilities in the prison, a large tank was brought in, and Susan was baptized. A minister's wife, assisting her, said later, "When Susan came up out of the water she said, 'Thank the Lord, I'm clean!' We were all crying. It was just too beautiful; . . . the joy on Susan's face was something to see. Since her conversion she has been a quiet witness in the prison." Susan wrote a friend on the outside:

"I am learning that love is the most important soul-winner. Without it I am nothing in God's hands. Love is patient and kind, and I pray that God will work out a plan so he can really love through me. . . . The hours I spend in Bible study and prayer each day strengthen me to meet the glares and gazes of those who are so skeptical, but who want to know what it is that has brought about a change in my life."

Sometimes it seems that a change of heart is more likely to take place when all of one's spiritual and emotional forces are brought into focus by a crisis. Have you noticed how much more fervently you pray when faced with some serious problem? In such circumstances one's diffused attention is narrowed down to a fine point. Simon Peter, sinking beneath the waves, cried out, "Lord, save me!" At that point he had a very short shopping list; he wanted only one thing. Thus one can be grateful for disasters and crises which sharpen our senses and tend to purify our motives. "But . . . you will seek the Lord your God, and you will find him, if you search after him with all your heart and with all your soul." [6]

10

Life Isn't Fair

> "No one ever makes any significant
> personal growth or achieves a measur-
> able change in personality, except as
> the result of the sharp stab of a crisis,
> or the dull throb of frustration."
> —Gabriel Montalban

Sheldon Kopp quotes a woman in a therapy group as saying, "I remember when I first discovered what life was like, I was furious. I guess I'm still kind of mad sometimes." [1]

I can identify with that. There are a thousand things about life which I dislike. I have no complaints for myself, but I cannot contemplate human or animal suffering without feeling a complex mixture of anger, compassion, and bewilderment that life should be so fraught with pain. I never see a TV or movie scene of a predator killing another animal without saying, "I *hate* that." The stark terror in the eyes of a fleeing zebra being brought down by a lion is enough to depress me for several hours.

Intellectually we all know that the predator must feed on its prey, but emotionally I identify with the victim. I bitterly resent killing, suffering, injustice, poverty, war, human deformity, pain, hunger, privation, disease, disaster, hardship or any aspect of life which brings sorrow to either humans or animals. In short, I hate suffering. I have been remarkably free from it myself, but I simply rebel against it for others.

As a boy I delighted in hunting. I winced a bit when I would pick up a dying rabbit I had shot, but the primitive million-year-old instinct of the hunter overcame it fairly easily then. Today I could not kill an animal. My first feeling after having killed an insect is always a flash of momentary sorrow that I have destroyed life. Some would view this as neurotic or ridiculous. So be it.

121

Why Is There Sin, Suffering and Sorrow?

I have no intention of trying to explain sin, suffering, and sorrow, that triumvirate of evil which has plagued the world from the beginning, for it is pretty generally recognized that this is one of God's mysteries. In the back of our minds we know that in the words of the old hymn, "Someday we'll understand." Meanwhile, we have a right to our human bewilderment.

Act of God or Accident?

A devastating earthquake destroys a city and thousands are killed or maimed. Insurance people call such a disaster "an act of God," which may be definitive enough for technical purposes, since it distinguishes such events from man-caused calamaties, but theologically it is a wretched label to attach to a natural disaster in no way "caused" by God.

During World War II many European cities were almost totally obliterated, and millions died in the holocaust, while other cities suffered little or no damage. One American family lost five sons in the war, while the son of a neighbor sat out the war in safety at the Pentagon. Life isn't fair.

Hurricanes, earthquakes and typhoons kill thousands nearly every year in various parts of the world with enormous loss of property. Does God guide the path of the hurricane so that it will destroy this town or city and not that one? We know the answer to that!

Epidemics, now largely under control, once decimated whole populations. Some died while others lived. By what capricious quirk, by what erratic, haphazard, illogical fate does an earthquake destroy churches and leave saloons and brothels standing?

Why are some people born into broken homes in the slums, while others are reared in prosperous, loving environments? A hundred thousand people lie down at night in the streets of Calcutta, having no home; nor will they ever have one. For them life is a frenzied struggle to earn, beg, or steal enough rice to maintain life. In Indonesia I saw hordes of homeless people eating, sleeping, breeding, bartering in the dust and mud of unpaved streets.

Who Do People Suffer?

In Kathmandu, Nepal, I saw my first leper. She was carrying a baby on her back. Her face was eaten away so badly that she wore a hideous grin. She begged piteously for coins. I was aware of a whole galaxy of emotions: sorrow and compassion, so that I wanted to give her everything I had; anger over the fact that there was nothing I could do to solve her problem; compassion for that tiny child she carried; and I was aware that other beggar-eyes were watching. When I gave her something I was suddenly besieged by the others. One was a woman suffering from elephantiasis, her legs horribly swollen into tree trunks. I escaped after emptying my pockets, with the same mixture of emotions I have felt in scores of cities all over the world where people suffer and beg and hurt and starve, and stare at the world with hungry, frightened eyes. Life isn't fair, and I hate its injustice!

Who Is to Blame?

Intellectually we sense that in the infinite wisdom of God, in his own time, all will be made right—we know not how. But at a feeling level I still hurt for the people suffering physically and emotionally, for whom I can do little or nothing.

In the pain of frustrated compassion, turned to anger over a blind fate that condemns people to suffer, there is a tendency to blame someone. I was once driving behind three boys on bicycles when one of them suddenly skidded, fell from his bike, and hit his head on the pavement. The other two boys and I gathered around him, and one of them said, "He lives right across the street in that house there." Foolishly, perhaps, I picked him up and carried him to the home the boys had pointed out. One of them rang the door bell. The mother came to the door, took in the scene with one horrified glance, and screamed at me, "You killed my boy!" Her maternal love and compassion had been instantly soured into venomous hostility by the human tendency to find the culprit first and ask questions later. The boy recovered from his slight concussion, I put him down, and he walked into the house.

There are no final answers. The answer to sin, suffering and sorrow—that triumvirate of evil—has not been given to us. Jesus promised us, not an absence of pain or sorrow, but quite the contrary. He assured us that "In the world you have tribulation; but be of good cheer, I have overcome the world." [2] By "overcoming the world" he cannot have meant that he had vanquished suffering and sorrow, which leaves one other alternative: he had faced the worst that life can do to a person—rejection, failure in achieving his announced purpose, the defection of his followers, and an agonizing and ignominious death. He had overcome all that life could hurl at him, and triumphed. He endured. I think he expects us to do that, too. The fact that life isn't fair is something over which we have no control. Undoubtedly, since we believe in the infinite love and justice of God, the scales will be balanced ultimately. In the interim, if there is suffering or grief or loss, dis-

appointment and discouragement, we can face it in the knowledge
that there is a time and place where God "will wipe away every
tear from their eyes, and death shall be no more, neither shall
there be mourning nor crying nor pain any more, for the former
things have passed away." [3]

Simplistic Answers Won't Do

"All well and good," replies a victim of poverty, discrimination
and sickness, to the non-sufferer quoting those glorious promises,
"but I desperately want some relief *in the here and now,* not in
the sky by and by. I'm hurting. I want some relief from the web
of circumstances which make life an unending crisis, and from
the physical and emotional stress that plagues me day and night.
The Bible says to 'ask, seek, knock,' and I've done that. I've prayed,
and read my Bible. I believe the Bible from cover to cover. Where
have I gone wrong? What's the answer?"

Would you care to answer that question? Without resorting to
worn cliches and hackneyed, simplistic solutions, can you provide
an answer that will satisfy and *comfort* that person?

Frankly, I *can't.* Some of God's mysteries await the final unveil-
ing. I don't pretend, meanwhile, to know all the answers, and I
don't know anyone who does.

The solutions I have discovered for my own life may not be
the ones which will fit the particular life situation of someone
else. I do know that life is not simple for many people. We are
all genetically, environmentally, and situationally different. Your
cure may not be mine, nor mine yours. We are at different points
in our growth toward wholeness. To say that "Christ is the answer"
may be no solution at all for an aged saint of God who has been
wracked with rheumatoid arthritis for thirty years, living with an
alcoholic husband and a mentally retarded child on an inadequate
pension. Try again. No, pious cliches and simplistic solutions will
not suffice. And when they come from people who have not genuinely suffered either severe emotional or physical pain, or tragic
losses, the over-simplified answers become more insult than solution.

Helps for Human Hurts

In the closing chapters of this book I have outlined briefly some
of the various methods and movements which have helped many
people. They may or may not help you, since each of us is so
radically different from everyone else. Yet, they are methods which
millions have found helpful. If you are hurting at some point, it
is my suggestion that you explore some of these possibilities.

The scripture, "Ask, and it will be given you; seek, and you will find; knock, and it will be opened to you," [4] suggests not a quick, simple, magical solution but rather a diligent, painstaking, disciplined search for a means of grace which will meet your particular needs. For some, because we are all limited in faith and perception, the search seems to take a long time. It took us a long time to get the way we are, and the cure may take a considerable amount of time, too. Spiritual and emotional growth toward wholeness was never intended to be an instant process. For growth, by its very nature, is always gradual. There is within each of us the growth principle. It is of God. That something within us—soul, spirit, God-self, divine spark of life—wants to grow, expand, and mature. We can help it best by providing the spiritual and emotional climate which will facilitate growth.

Whether it be a worship service, meditation technique, Primal Integration, Lay Witness, the charismatic experience, or some other avenue, the important thing is to get into motion. Find the emphasis or method which best suits your personality and background and individual needs. "For it is God who works in you, inspiring both the will and the deed, for his own chosen purpose." [5]

It is safe to say that we shall probably never understand, in this life, the mystery of suffering and sorrow; but even with our limited knowledge it is possible to sense certain positive aspects of pain, recognizing meanwhile that there are a thousand unknowns. This poem offers, if not an explanation for the origin of grief and tragedy, some insight into the by-products of human sorrow and pain.

> Why must I be hurt?
> Suffering and despair,
> Cowardice and cruelty,
> Envy and injustice.
> All these hurt.
> Grief and terror,
> Loneliness and betrayal
> And the agony of loss or death—
> All these things hurt.
> Why? Why must life hurt?
> Why must those who love generously,
> Live honorably, feel deeply
> All that is good and beautiful
> Be so hurt, while selfish creatures
> Go unscathed?
> That is why—because they can feel.
> Hurt is the price to pay for feeling,
> Pain is not an accident,
> Nor punishment, nor mockery

By some savage god.
Pain is a part of growth.
The more we grow the more we feel.
The more we feel—the more we suffer.
For if we are able to feel beauty
We must also feel the lack of it.
Those who glimpse heaven
Are bound to sight hell.
To have felt deeply is worth
Anything it costs.
To have felt love and honor
Is worth any price.
And so—since hurt is the price
Of larger living, I will not
Hate pain, nor try to escape it.
Instead I will try to meet it
Bravely, bear it proudly:
Not as a cross or misfortune, but an
Opportunity, a privilege, a challenge—
To the God who gropes within me.
—Elsie Robinson

This poem is beautiful, insightful and helpful—up to a point. But I doubt if it would comfort the several hundred thousand victims of torture in South American distatorships, or elsewhere; nor would it prove particularly inspiring to a person doubled up in pain or dying in agony. Run-of-the-mill pain or disappointment or even death I can accept with equanimity—I have no problem there. But what of calculated brutality, sadistic acts resulting in terror and agony?

A weekly newsmagazine carried the shocking account of parents whose small daughter dropped her coat on the floor. As punishment she was forced to drink enormous quantities of water as a reminder not to repeat the offense. She died in agony. Her suffering had no redeeming value.

In a lengthy series of counseling sessions I listened to the story of a woman, born illegitimate, who was reared in a sociological garbage dump. The alcoholic mother told the child repetitiously through the years, "I told your father I'd go ahead and have the baby, but I'd never love it, and I never *will* love you. *No* one will ever love you. Get out of my sight! I can't stand to look at you! You'll never get any love from me or anyone else." This was not an angry outburst in a moment of exasperation, but the message the child received as a daily verbal diet for years. While it is relatively easy to see that a certain amount of disappointment and pain can motivate us and stimulate personal growth, no one

can convince me that there is any value to be derived from such
sadism directed at a little child.

Does God "Take" Our Loved Ones?

In an effort to make sense out of senseless slaughter, irrational
and stupid acts of cruelty and injustice, people are sometimes
driven to make ridiculous statements, such as: "God took your
Daddy," or "God needs children in heaven, too, which is why he
took your child." Such statements are not true and can cause
enormous pain and misunderstanding.

There is value to be derived from learning to endure disappointment and suffering; but to say, "suffering is good for you," to a
person who has endured weeks or months of physical and mental
torture would be likely to get you a slap in the face, or worse.
And such action would be justified.

Platitudes will not comfort a mother whose husband and five
children are killed when a drunk driver runs into their car.
There is no way one can make any sense out of that! To try to
spiritualize it is not an act of kindness. The sufferer needs love and
understanding, not pat explanations.

Life simply isn't fair. Something within us aches with a great
longing for justice, for a happy ending, for "all the bad people
to be good, and the good people to be nice," as one little girl
expressed it in a beautiful prayer.

Are you getting depressed? Would you rather read something
uplifting, inspiring, cheerful? I would prefer to relate only happy,
exciting, victorious events, where everything turns out all right
in the end. But that isn't life, which happens to consist, for some
reason, of sadness and pain as well as happiness and joy. So, let's
see what we can make of this illogical, mysterious world where
very often the righteous suffer while the wicked prosper.

Is God in Charge?

In a therapy group I was conducting, a woman asked, "If God is
in charge of this world, how do you account for the injustice and
suffering we see all about us?" I replied, "God is not in charge of
this world. We are. The Bible tells us that God said, 'Let us
make man in our image, after our likeness; and let them have
dominion over the fish of the sea, and over the birds of the air, . . .
and over all the earth. . . .' [6] *God is not running things on this
earth. We are in charge of the whole operation!* God's resources
are available to us, but we are the ones responsible. Furthermore,"
I added, "Jesus refers three times in one brief discourse to Satan
as 'the ruler of this world.' " [7] In one of his letters the Apostle

Paul refers to "the prince of the power of the air, the spirit that is now at work in the sons of disobedience." [8] No, God is not in charge. *We* are. And what a miserable mess we have made of it!

To ascribe the horrors of war, the battering of little children by their parents, and the ten thousand varieties of human sorrow and suffering to God is blasphemous. True, he *permits* it, but he does not *cause* it. Why does he permit it? The answer seems obvious. If he is going to give us free will, then this permits a drunken driver to run down a sweet little old lady on her way to church. Free will allows a Hitler to flourish, or a Stalin to exterminate an estimated thirty million people in his lust for power. [9] If I am to have freedom of choice, then all other humans must also have it; and that permits evil or weak or careless people to bring untold suffering into the lives of others.

Does Suffering Make Us Wise?

In an effort to try to make sense out of human suffering people reach for all manner of wild explanations, such as the idea that suffering produces wisdom. If that were true all the world would be wise, for everyone suffers to some degree. Seneca once said that "Life itself is neither good nor evil, it is the *scene* of good and evil."

Paul points out in his letter to the Christians at Rome that, "We rejoice in our sufferings, knowing that suffering produces endurance, and endurance produces character, and character produces hope. . . . " [10] Paul was using the editorial "we" in his letter. That had been *his* experience, but I am confident that he would not imply that *all* suffering is character-building.

I have seen the slums of a score or more of the great cities of the world and I doubt sincerely if anyone would claim that such degrading, abysmal poverty was producing strong character and wisdom. We know, as a matter of fact, that in most instances it breeds every conceivable kind of crime and character distortion.

Why War?

Marine Sergeant Leonard Koontz who came under intensive fire in Viet Nam, tells about his wartime experience: "A friend of mine and I were moving up a hill. He was a good friend of mine. He got hit in the stomach with a .50 caliber machine gun. . . . I ran up the hill to get him. I grabbed him by the legs, . . . and his legs came off in my hands. He sat up and looked at the legs in my hands and said, 'Lenny, *why?*' "

Yes, *why?* Why his friend, and not Lenny? Why does *anyone* have to die that way?

At Luxor, about four hundred miles up the Nile from Cairo, we met one of the happiest young men I have ever known. I still remember his radiantly beautiful smile. He lived in abject poverty in a tiny mud village close to some ancient ruins. At one point he asked with a look of infinite wistfulness if we could take him back with us to the United States. It was impossible, of course, but how I longed to bring this beautiful young man home with us.

Soon after returning home, I had lunch in San Francisco at the Palace Hotel with a friend who arrived with an aggrieved look on his face. He sat down and erupted angrily: "I was late because I had to go to the bank and get some stock out of my safety deposit box so I could sell it and pay my income taxes." I said, "Too bad, but you still have a couple of million left, don't you?"

"Sure! But I hate digging into my stocks this way." He was miserable. I thought of the smiling young man at Luxor, and then looked at the sullen face of my friend.

Why, despite grinding poverty are some people able to remain cheerful, while others are miserable in their prosperity?

Why Evil?

During World War II British Intelligence cracked the German code. From 1939 onward Churchill, Roosevelt, Eisenhower and other Allied leaders were virtually reading over Hitler's shoulder. Sometimes translated copies of Hitler's orders to his generals were in Allied hands within an hour of the original transmission.

On November 4, 1940, the British picked up German bombing orders for a blitz of the cathedral city of Coventry well before the attack was due. Word was relayed to Churchill, who then faced a terrible decision; whether to evacuate Coventry and almost certainly give their secret to the Germans. He decided to let Coventry die. The city, including its inhabitants and treasures, was virtually wiped from the face of the earth.

Why Coventry? Why war, devastation, pillage, rape and murder? Why sickness and disease and epidemics? Why evil?

An estimated six million Jews (and even more refugees from other Eastern European nations who are seldom mentioned) were driven from their homes and exterminated. Surviving Jews then drove nearly two million peaceful Palestinian Arabs from their homes. Why?

American Indians were once exterminated like vermin, the remnant finally herded into reservations, often in scrubby desert land. A UN Commission estimated that thirty million Chinese were systematically slaughtered when the Communists took over. The list of known atrocities would fill a book. The mind finally rebels and refuses to be shocked any longer by statistics. But the people who suffer or die are not statistics; they are human beings, who hurt, bleed and die. Why should it be them instead of other people half a continent away?

These are unanswerable questions. Any of our rationalizations are just that—an effort to make rational the irrational actions of human beings.

Some Overcome Handicaps

Some people summon strength to overcome the handicap of a deprived childhood, or emotional or situational problem. Peter Ilyich Tchaikovsky, the greatest and most prolific of all Russian composers, was a tragic and troubled figure throughout most of his life. He suffered a series of emotional breakdowns during his life, and on at least one occasion attempted suicide. Yet, strangely enough, despite his personal tragedies, Tchaikovsky's music is the most romantic and popular, perhaps the most triumphant and stirring ever composed.

Robert Schumann, the German composer, whose music is noted for its great poetic beauty, died in an insane asylum. Franz Schubert, one of the most prolific of composers, lived only thirty-one years, always in the most abject poverty, supported largely by friends. Most of his work was not published until after his death. He died unknown, unhonored and unsung, a pauper.

Why the pain, the sorrow, the injustice, the age-long human suffering? The anguished cry comes down the lengthening corridors of time—why? And there is only a silence that echoes through the ages.

Life Is Not Neat or Logical

The human mind likes neat, logical explanations which will relieve anxiety. An American journalist in the Middle East was walking along the street with a prominent Moslem when they heard the startling news that a beloved national leader had just been assassinated. The Moslem stopped in shock and unbelief, and then said in Arabic, *"Inshallah."* (Variously translated, "if God wills it," or "as God wills it," or "the will of God," depending on the circumstances.) The American said, "That was an assassination, not the will of God." His friend replied, "If I did not believe in the will of God behind everything, I would lose my mind." But ascribing human tragedy to the *intentional* will of God would surely not be in harmony with the spirit or teachings of Christ, who said, "It is not the will of my Father who is in heaven that one of these little ones should perish." [11]

Some years ago hundreds of children around the world suffered horrible birth defects and deformities as the result of their mothers' having taken the drug Thalidomide. Some were born without arms or legs, or with flippers at the elbows for arms, and tragically deformed heads and bodies. Vast sums, running into the millions, were finally awarded the parents by the company which manufactured the drug; but this could not remedy the awful tragedy. Would any thoughtful person care to fit this horror into the *intentional* will of God?

God Allows But Does Not Cause Evil

My emphasis on the *intentional* will of God brings us inevitably to the consideration of different aspects of God's will. It is important to distinguish between the *intentional* will of God, and his *permissive* will.

When our son was sixteen and had secured his driver's license I rode with him a few times after he had taken driver's training. I observed that he had "shot gun" or tunnel vision, with little or no awareness of what was happening to the right or left. I pointed this out to him and was rewarded with the kind of defensive grunt one would expect from a normal, lovable, rotten, adolescent. I said, "When you go out on your date tonight, I am going to go home and pray."

"What about?" he asked.

"That you will not injure yourself or anyone else. The car is insured, but I'm worried about that tunnel vision of yours." Another grunt. I did pray—earnestly. At 11:30 there came a frantic telephone call. Breathlessly a very humble young man was panting, "Dad! I wrecked the car!"

"Anyone hurt?" I asked.

"No, but both cars are wrecked—totalled."

"Glory to God," I replied, grateful that no one had been killed or injured. My prayer had been answered.

Just in passing I may mention that the young man, greatly chastened, thereafter became a very careful driver. He had learned something very important which no mere adult could have taught him.

Did the fact that he "learned something" mean that God sent the accident so he could learn a lesson? Obviously not. I have heard sincere and otherwise intelligent Christians tell how the death of someone's child had brought the parents closer to the Lord, so it must have been God's will for the child to die. Preposterous! And worse, blasphemous. God does not kill children to get the parents' attention.

Parents Also Allow Free Will for Children

Now, when I permitted my son to drive a car, knowing that he

stood a fairly good chance, ultimately, of having an accident, I
was not intentionally working out a plan whereby he would "learn
a lesson" through an accident. But in my *permissive* will he took
charge of a car, just as Adam assumed responsibility in the Garden.
And, even as Adam, he blew it. God gave Adam and Eve free will;
they were free to obey God or to ignore his commands. This frightful freedom which we cherish so deeply is a very costly gift.

Dr. Leslie Weatherhead, for many years the pastor of London's
City Temple, lists three specific aspects of the will of God: [12]

1. The *intentional* will of God.
2. The *circumstantial* will of God.
3. The *ultimate* will of God.

He points out the fallacy of trying to make the phrase "The will
of God" fit all three. For instance, as Weatherhead points out, it
was surely not the original intention of God that Jesus should die
in agony on the cross. Prophecy (foreseeing and announcing a
future event) does not necessarily imply that the event foretold is
the *intentional* will of God. Jesus came with the intention that
men should follow and obey him. The repentance and conversion
of Israel was the intentional will of God, not the death of Jesus.

Why Are Missionaries Not Divinely Protected?

Some years ago a group of dedicated missionaries in South
America decided to try to win the Auca Indians, a hostile neigh-
boring tribe. In the process, the missionaries were all slaughtered.
Who would wish to call this horrible event the intentional will of
God? God permitted it, but did not cause it.

The widow of one of the missionaries ultimately made friends
with the Auca Indians and, with her little daughter, went to live
among them. The Indians felt no threat from a mother and child
and readily accepted them. Here is an instance of the circumstantial will of God—under the circumstances, the courage and Christian love of the missionary's widow resulted in some wonderfully
creative and thrilling results. But surely no one in his right mind
would care to state that God "willed" the husband to die so the
wife and infant daughter could successfully complete the task of
evangelizing the Auca Indians.

A child wanders away from home, explores a neighbor's yard,
falls into the swimming pool, and drowns. It was not the will of
God that the child should wander away, nor that the telephone
should ring at the precise moment the child decided to roam,
momentarily distracting the mother's attention. But once the
natural curiosity of the child is in operation, and the child falls
into the pool, it is God's *circumstantial* will that the law of gravity

shall operate as usual—that the child's lungs shall fill with water, and death take place by drowning. God permits disaster, but does not cause it. It is not a part of God's plan that universal laws shall be suspended in order that a child, or a nation for that matter, shall survive. These "natural" laws—laws of physics, chemistry, biology, etc.—are universal in application. They are actually divine laws and are not suspended erratically, or magically, in order that we shall always be spared death, pain or sorrow.

By the *ultimate* will of God is meant that in the end, nothing can defeat the glorious purposes and intention of God. Man's sin or stupidity or carelessness may temporarily delay the final working out of the ultimate design of God, but cannot defeat it. There are a thousand mysteries and imponderables, but we know how it all turns out in the end, when "the kingdom of the world has become the kingdom of our Lord and of his Christ, and he shall reign for ever and ever." [13]

John Greenleaf Whittier, in his poem "The Eternal Goodness," has expressed his simple trust in the unseen purposes of God:

> I know not where his islands
> Lift their fronded palms in air;
> I only know I cannot drift
> Beyond his love and care.

11

Fear, Anxiety and Wholeness

> "I write to make you afraid. I myself
> am a man who is afraid. All the wise
> men I know are afraid."
> —Harold Urey, Nobel Prize winner
> and one of the scientists whose
> work led to the atom bomb

In 1938 a German with great foresight perceived that undoubtedly the world would soon be plunged into another world war. With infinite patience and Teutonic thoroughness he explored all of the possibilities for survival and finally determined, after exhaustive research, to take his family to a lovely island and start life anew before the impending holocaust.

The family settled in their new island home with the calm assurance that their farsightedness had spared them the rigors and horrors of war. A few years later they discovered that there is no place to hide. The island they chose was Guadalcanal, where some of the fiercest fighting ever to take place on this planet occurred.

Fear As a Survival Factor

Fortunately, more often than not, the God-given survival aspect of fear does pay off. A modest amount of fear, in the form of caution, can prevent one from walking casually into heavy traffic. It can keep one from investing impetuously in every get-rich-quick scheme that comes along. The knowledge that this or that particular decision has proven harmful or disastrous to others can alert one to the possibility of suffering the same fate. Fear, caution, anxiety—all varying aspects of the same basic emotion—are fundamentally life-saving, survival-oriented instincts. Properly used, a moderate amount of this emotion can save us individually, and perhaps collectively, from disaster.

In excess, fear can inhibit, paralyze, and so limit one as to make life a tension-ridden ordeal. I think of two men in their mid-forties who were in a therapy group I conducted. Both suffered from phobias of a similar nature. A person who has never suffered from a severe phobia cannot have the slightest concept of what a terrifying and disabling thing it is. Phobia is defined as an exaggerated, usually inexplicable and irrational fear of some particular object or class of objects, or of certain places or experiences. This fear usually has been displaced from some buried memory or emotion onto something less threatening, but still frightening.

One of the men suffered from agoraphobia, fear of open places; but his case was much more encompassing than the definitive term suggests. He could not travel anywhere except from home to work without suffering a paralyzing panic. If rush hour traffic slowed to a stop, in a moment or two he would be seized with unreasoning terror so great that he felt an almost uncontrollable urge to leap from the car and run.

The other man suffering from a phobia feared to cross bridges. When it became necessary to cross either the San Francisco Golden Gate Bridge or the Bay Bridge, his panic seemed to know no bounds. These men were both Christians, well aware of the Scripture often quoted to them by well-meaning but uncomprehending friends, "Perfect love casts out fear;" [1] but the admonitions to think positively, trust more, put it out of your mind, only served to compound the problem by making them feel more guilty. Both were relatively passive individuals, who tended to bury their hostility. By repressing their legitimate anger toward friends or relatives with simplistic solutions, their depression worsened, and thus their phobias increased. Eventually, through extensive therapy, both largely overcame their phobias, and began to live more normal lives.

Phobias are usually very difficult to eradicate, for the roots go very deep. Most people, fortunately, do not suffer from irrational fears of that magnitude; but a host of people experience undue tension, induced by excessive anxiety; and this tension is one aspect of stress, which is the single greatest cause of virtually all illness.

Specific and Generalized Fear

Often it is not one big fear that causes undue tension. Many individuals suffer from a generalized anxiety and tension induced by nameless small fears: fear of not performing well, thus of failing; fear of ridicule, of rejection, of being late; fear of a marriage failure, of being a poor parent; fear of financial insecurity, etc. In millions of people, nameless little unknown fears add up to migraine or tension headaches, a tightened stomach, gastrointestinal problems, nervousness, or psychogenic fatigue, which is simply an excessive fatigue with no discernable cause. This type of fatigue is usually induced by living under long-term tension or stress. Many people have lived that way all of their lives and have never known anything else.

Dr. Paul Tournier comments on this generalized type of fear: "The result is a world which is afraid. Without God, fear rules: fear with its two sets of reactions, the strong ones, such as bravado, aggressiveness, injustice; and the weak, such as panic, cowardice, and flight. The result is universal war. We know that science owes its upswing in large part to man's desire to escape from fear. To master nature, to understand in order not to have fear any longer, to banish mystery, this is what science has been striving to do." [2]

There are innumerable causes of all-pervasive anxiety. A child who received little or no cuddling and holding often becomes an adult with a vague, diffused, generalized anxiety, which may manifest itself in many ways such as tension, phobias, unreasoning hostility, a judgmental and critical attitude, physical symptoms, generalized fatigue, alcoholism, over-eating, over-working, etc. Each person has a different genetic wiring, and a multitude of differences exist in the way any two children are treated and the ways they respond. Or, alternating love and rejection can generate the same kind of anxiety.

Excessiveness Is Rooted in Childhood

Most of the roots of excessiveness go back to childhood, but occasionally there is a monumental fear or disabling phobia which seems to have a later origin. Miriam is a case in point. In a series of primal sessions she was regressed to childhood and relived a series of sexual molestation experiences with two uncles, a grandfather, and last of all to surface—with an enormous mixture of fear, guilt and horror—a sexual encounter with her own father. Now she knew why she had never wanted her father to touch her as an adult. Reliving these events seemed to discharge most of the nameless anxiety which she had experienced for many years; but finally she relived an event at age twenty which had a bearing on a previously unexplained fear of great intensity.

She played the organ at her church, and though she was a very competent musician and had no conscious fear of disapproval or criticism from any source, she always finished the service with an unreasoning panic. She told me:

"In one primal I got into the deep humiliation and hurt I had experienced when I was twenty years old. It turned out to be an incident which I remembered, but I had buried the intense hurt it had caused. I returned to college after having a baby and felt very vulnerable and apprehensive about going back. As a music student, one of my professors publicly embarrassed me. I didn't finish the semester and I drummed up an excuse for dropping out. I never knew why I did that until I got into that primal and relived it. I know now why I always have such fear when performing publicly, especially in the realm of music—for it was a music teacher who humiliated me, and I developed a deep fear of being inadequate. I reexperienced the fear of shame and hurt in the primal session."

Insight Is Not Enough

An intellectual awareness of why we do something irrational, or have an excessive reaction, seldom solves the problem. In order to eradicate forever a deeply rooted fear or phobia it is usually necessary to relive the precipitating event with as much emotional intensity as the original event. (This is discussed in more detail in the last chapter under Primal Integration.)

A friend of mine, a highly effective and successful minister, told me humorously when he turned down a call to one of the largest churches in his denomination, "I have a hysterical fear of failure. I don't want to become a nationally known failure." His fear served as a brake on an ambition which was slightly greater than his abilities, and he was aware of this limitation.

People Who Cannot Acknowledge Fear

There are people who are counter-phobic. That is, they engage in dare-devil exploits or take unnecessary risks, in an unconscious effort to prove to themselves and others that they are not afraid. Without in any way disparaging these people, it can be pointed out that race car drivers, mountain climbers, parachute jumpers, and all excessive risk-takers are motivated by the two-fold need to prove that they are not afraid and to experience the momentary thrill that comes when danger threatens.

A slightly built, rather passive, timid young man told me with great openness and candor why he had joined the Marines. "I got little or no love as a child. I had always been timid and afraid and doubted my manhood; so, as soon as I was old enough I joined the Marines, because their ads appealed to my sense of insecurity and doubts about my masculinity. I guess I thought it would make a man out of me."

Undoubtedly there are thousands of parachute jumpers, hang gliders, mountain climbers, and assorted chance-takers who are not aware of great fear when engaging in their exploits. They insist that they take part in these activities for the thrill. Subconsciously they are *denying* fear.

A young minister came to see me about some personal problems. He was performing very inadequately in his church and exhibited significant signs of emotional immaturity and deep anxiety. He brought with him a large reel of color movies taken of him while he was making innumerable parachute jumps. He insisted that my staff and I should see the movies before we engaged in any discussion of his personal problems. He was not consciously aware of fear. Inwardly he was a quaking mass of insecurities and anxiety, which manifested themselves in compulsive talking and nervous habits. He discharged his anxieties temporarily by making weekly parachute jumps.

The "act as if" principle will work to some degree, in certain cases. That is, if you are afraid, and act as if you are not, in time the feelings can catch up with the actions. For instance, one can overcome a fear of public speaking, or any similar experience, by acting on the simple principle of "doing the thing you fear to do." This will work for that particular situation, but not necessarily for others.

Fear of Heights

For instance, I have always had a mild but irritating fear of heights. It does not interfere with my life in the slightest, except that I avoid getting on tall ladders. On my first plane flight many years ago I was paralyzed with fear. On subsequent flights the fear gradually diminished, until it was dissipated entirely—so far as planes are concerned. But ladders? No, I still get dizzy if I get very far up on one. Conquering a fear of heights on a plane five miles high did not carry over to solving my fear of being on a ladder five *feet* up in the air.

Fear and anxiety are not always clear-cut emotions. On occasion one can experience a whole galaxy of feelings and find difficulty in sorting and labelling them. (Mixed emotions are very common, as in the case of the parents who were waiting up until 4:00 A.M. for their sixteen-year-old daughter to come home from a date. At 4:15 she came in blithely—with a Gideon Bible under her arm!)

Mixed emotions, a kind of all pervasive ambivalence, create a great deal of anxiety and tension. Jesus makes it clear that "No servant can serve two masters; for either he will hate the one and love the other, or he will be devoted to the one and despise the other. You cannot serve God and mammon." [3] The principle involved here concerns emotions and spiritual ambivalence. Kierkegaard has pointed out that purity of heart is to will one thing, meaning singleness of purpose as opposed to divided loyalties. Having a divided allegiance to two masters, or a split devotion to God and material possessions, is impossible to tolerate without generating deep anxiety. It is not an offense to God primarily, but is damaging to the person trying to split his loyalties, his energy, or his ultimate goals.

Divided Loyalties Produce Anxiety

One of the devastating results of such a split is anxiety. It is tension-producing to want two different things with almost equal intensity. It places undue strain on the psychic forces of the individual. A *schizophrenic* is simply a person, by definition, who has "split." The term is often applied quite loosely to any seriously disturbed individual, but basically schizophrenia implies a split personality. Often it is the result of striving with equal strength to try to meet two opposing goals or demands. A woman who desperately wants to marry a man who has proposed, but is in a state of conflict because her parents insist she stay and help support the family, is placed in an intolerable position through no fault of her own. I recall a son whose mother, a widow, referred to him at age six, as "my little man." Later she called him "my substitute husband," thinking that she was bestowing love. Each time he made plans to marry, his mother became seriously ill. This happened so many times he became at first suspicious, then angry. Loyalty to his mother and the legitimate need to establish his own home were in conflict, and it was only through extensive counseling that he was able to cut the cord with which his mother had bound him and be freed of his great anxiety.

Finding the Source of Your Conflict

Whatever is pulling you apart, whatever is causing conflict in your life, needs to be examined openly and honestly with a competent counselor. Friends can give you advice ranging from the absurd to the ridiculous, often damaging, occasionally valid. Only a competent, objective, emotionally uninvolved counselor can assist you in resolving a serious conflict.

Sometimes ambivalence creates great anxiety, because to take either choice involves emotional pain or guilt. I recall a man who loved and needed his wife, but who fell in love with a woman a few miles down the street who seemed to meet certain needs in his life. He actually set up two households and had a child by the second woman. Of course, the duplicity was ultimately discovered, and a divorce ensued. Irrationally, he had pleaded with his wife to understand and to permit him to live in both households! The conflict engendered in his life resulted in all manner of aberrations: business failure, poor judgment, increasing tension and anxiety.

An executive could not be equally loyal to both Ford and General Motors. Each has secrets from the other. One who is living a lie has the same problem, only intensified, for he is not only a divided personality, but is living with a load of guilt; and guilt is probably the most destructive human emotion. Sin and guilt are not "bad" just because God says so. God says so because it is true. God is against whatever is destructive to us, his children, for he loves us. All commandments and teachings, from the Ten Commandments to the principles enunciated by Jesus, are simply universal, cosmic laws which we disobey to our own destruction. Anxiety, tension, emotional and physical symptoms result when the conflict becomes too great.

A whole person has learned to live with the least possible amount of inner conflict, is steadfastly determined to make the choices and decisions which will be in harmony with his or her basic moral principles, and has been "cleaned out" of any devastating childhood influences which have seriously marred the personality.

A Traumatic Childhood Causes Anxiety

Sometimes one is not whole until damaging early influences have been dealt with. Often if there were childhood traumas, the end result is conflict and gnawing, devastating anxiety. The symptoms can range all the way from mild anxiety-producing tension to a disabling neurosis. A woman whose physical symptoms finally drove her to search for traumas which might have caused the damage, engaged in a series of primal sessions with me. Her marriage was in ruins, because she could not give or receive love. She had numerous memories of her bitter, angry mother, and her loving but passive father, but she was not prepared for the vivid scenes which unfolded before her, and which she relived with great intensity. Her mother firmly believed that a child must be beaten regularly in order to maintain discipline, and she reexperienced those traumatic events with tears and pleadings week after week.

After one such session I asked, "Where was Daddy when you needed him to protect you?" There was a moment's pause, and then a barrage of anger was expressed toward her father who, in his weakness, had gone along with the daily punishment being meted out. As a child she had "shut down" on her feelings in order to survive. Now, in order to live fully she had to get in touch with those buried emotions and relive them. As she did so, in session after session, she found herself more and more willing to try it again with her husband, from whom she was separated; for as the repressed anguish was discharged, she became able to give and receive love in a far more mature way.

The Parent-Tape and Anxiety

Though the details are sketchy in my conscious mind, I felt a need to be incessantly in motion if I were to appease my parents and win their approval. Although I surely had ample time to play and was not seriously mistreated (except through frequent heavy-handed physical punishment) the basic feeling which I brought into adult life was, "I must never sit down, never rest; I must always be busy, productive." That message is inscribed on my nervous system and has nothing to do with an enlightened conscious mind which recognizes the truth that rest and recreation are important. I feel guilty if someone sees me resting. My intellect comes to the rescue but fails to stifle the condemnation of my inner judicial system, which demands that I be in constant motion. The parent-tape, though very strong, is somewhat muted. I am not totally under its control. I can defy it, but my feeling is that in some degree the tape will go on playing endlessly. Many people suffer from this irrational drive to be constantly busy. It is the basic urge which keeps all workaholics going full steam ahead, without let-up.

There is a mistaken idea that Jesus said, "The truth shall make you free." I have seen that statement engraved on the portals of universities and libraries. That is not precisely what he said. In its entirety the passage read, *"If you continue in my word, you are truly my disciples,* and you will know the truth, and the truth will make you free."* [4] (Author's italics). The New English Bible reads, "If you dwell within the revelation I have brought, you are indeed my disciples; you shall know the truth, and the truth will set you free." The usual interpretation, which just isn't true, is that if you get enough facts in your head you will be freed of all your hang-ups and limitations. Plenty of highly educated people with a vast store-house of information, both sacred and secular, have enormous hang-ups of all kinds. Many of them can testify that the mere acquisition of facts does not necessarily make one a free person in any sense.

Does Truth Make One Free?

Jesus makes it clear that *if one lives according to the full revela-*

tion which he brought, that enables such a person to be his disciple, who is then *eligible to know the truth.* This is no small requirement! It involves vastly more than memorizing a host of Scripture verses and making a profession of faith. Intellectual "truth" is not sufficient.

This is why just becoming aware of the origin of a problem does not guarantee a cure. A compulsive worker goes to his physician who tells him, "You are working too hard. You must get more rest and exercise, and follow this diet I am going to give you." The instructions and insight are important, but now begins the hard part: to break the power of a parent-tape running incessantly in the patient's head; to get rid of the anxiety that drives him mercilessly; to develop motivation sufficiently to rest more, to exercise, and to stay on a diet. Ah! Carrying out that task is different, for it involves discipline, effort, and the reprogramming of his emotional structure. It may take a long time to effect a change.

A nervous, uptight woman whose compulsive talking betrays her inner anxiety, is told by her psychologist to "relax, take things easier, don't be so tense, slow down your speech," but it is useless counsel unless something is done to eradicate the roots of her inner distress, which go back into her distant childhood. Insight is seldom enough if the anxiety is deep.

It can be demonstrated that every action we take, large or small, is basically an effort to relieve anxiety, whether it be the act of uncrossing your legs (thus relieving the physical tension-anxiety caused by shutting off the blood supply) or getting out of bed to dress and go to work (thus avoiding the anxiety produced by the thought of being late or of not showing up for work at all). A mild anxiety is productive. It is the activating principle behind every action. When the anxiety becomes severe it is then counterproductive, for it generates stress, which in time can produce manifold physical and emotional symptoms.

Children in a Hostile World

Psychiatrist Karen Horney developed a concept of basic anxiety which she described as feelings of helplessness in a potentially hostile world. She felt that basic anxiety developed as the result of the feeling of hostility evoked by rejecting or impatient parents. In childhood these feelings are aroused by such parental attitudes as preferences for other children, reproaches the child considers unjust, unpredictable changes in discipline—being over-indulgent and then rejecting. For the child, little and weak as compared to his powerful parents, is in no position to rebel and must bury his feelings of anger or frustration. The repressed anger generates anxiety in later life.

Dr. Louis Gluck, professor of pediatrics at the Yale School of Medicine, believes that the mother's state of mind during pregnancy has a vast deal to do with the child's early emotional reactions. If the mother experiences significant anxiety, fear or apprehension during pregnancy she will probably have a fussy child with eating problems. The infant born to an anxious mother becomes an adult who may be tense, anxious, and suffer from a generalized free-floating anxiety, but never able to pinpoint the source of his tension.

Anxiety and Shyness

One aspect of fear seldom dealt with is the matter of shyness. A team of psychologists [5] made a study of students at Stanford University and came up with some startling findings. Forty percent of the students described themselves as shy and indicated a need for some kind of therapy to get them out of their prison. There were seven aspects of their shyness which, incidentally, does not always diminish or disappear as one grows older. These seven are:
1. Difficulty in meeting new people and making friends.
2. Negative reactions such as depression, isolation and loneliness.
3. Reluctance in being properly assertive or expressing opinions.
4. Presenting a confusing picture of themselves to others, making it difficult for other people to perceive the shy person's real assets.
5. Unwittingly presenting a picture of themselves as snobbish, indifferent, cold, unfriendly or weak.
6. Difficulty in thinking clearly and communicating effectively in the presence of others.
7. A self-conscious and excessive preoccupation with their own feelings and reactions.

Physical Symptoms of Shyness

The abnormally shy person experiences a kind of modified terror, involving increased pulse rate, blushing, excessive perspiration, tightening of the stomach muscles, and pounding heart. Such a person may be evidencing complete poise, or at least be motionless on the outside, but inwardly is suffering painfully. In a number of instances the exceptionally shy person was perceived by others as being condescending, aloof, bored or hostile. These outward manifestations, of course, are the result of an effort to cover up the feelings of inadequacy and fear that are aroused by the presence of others.

I recall reading a sermon some years ago by one of the nation's most famous ministers in which he stated that shyness and self-consciousness are simply the result of excessive vanity and preoccupation with oneself. He proposed that such people should

change at once and become more outgoing and less vain; which is
on a par with telling a person with a broken leg to "snap out of it.
You're just preoccupied with your own pain."

Another study at the University of California revealed that teenagers who were often the least talkative, the least animated and
assertive, but responsible and cooperative, were the most tense.
They were bottling up their inner tumult for the sake of acceptance. None of them appeared to be aware of the surging inner
turmoil, having lived with this anxiety-producing tension all of
their lives.

At this point, the more or less standard practice is to give you
ten simple steps which will enable you to get rid of any shyness,
inferiority feelings, anxiety, tension and excessive fear in a very
short time. I really wish that this were possible. But, my friend,
to outline a simple procedure to solve those problems would simply
make matters worse for you, by inducing guilt; for when you found
out that the ten easy steps are really not easy, you would feel less
adequate and more guilty than ever. It would please me mightily
if there were a sure-fire, guaranteed, quick cure for emotional and
spiritual ailments. There isn't.

Growth is a slow process. Trees and people do not grow by leaps
and bounds, but imperceptibly. It seems to be God's way. But there
is hope. In the last chapters are listed, with brief descriptions, a
number of outstanding movements which are specializing in changing lives, and doing it successfully.

Simplistic Solutions

"Why can't everyone be healed through hearing the gospel and
accepting Christ? Why are there so many different denominations
and such a variety of religious movements? It would all be so
simple if everyone would just trust the Lord and cast all their
burdens on him." Thus spoke a young minister's wife in a counseling session. I asked, "How is it with you? You have been a Christian all your life; are you all healed up, whole, at peace with God,
yourself and everyone else?"

"No, I'm not. You know that! But I think I'm angry because
life is so complicated. It ought to be simpler."

"Right; but it isn't. Your inner child of the past is asking for
magic; for a Celestial Daddy to make everything right with one
wave of his hand."

"Yes, my Daddy was like that. He fixed everything."

"Well," I said, "God doesn't work like that, much as we might
like for him to. He seems to have some plan whereby we are to
grow through diligent search, continuity, discipline and effort." She

nodded, giving intellectual assent, while her inner child looked very unhappy.

I have no simplistic solutions, but as you will see before we conclude this book, there are ways and means by which thousands of people have found a growing maturity and wholeness. If you are sufficiently motivated—which is usually the result of the sharp stab of a crisis or the dull throb of frustration—you will very likely begin an earnest search for new dimensions of spiritual growth, through one or more of the movements described in the final chapters.

12

Do You Really Want
to Be a Whole Person?

> "Just as the physician might say that
> there lives perhaps not one single man
> who is in perfect health, so one might
> say perhaps there lives not one single
> man who after all is not to some ex-
> tent in despair, in whose inmost parts
> there does not dwell a disquietude, a
> perturbation, a discord, an anxious
> dread of an unknown something. . . . "
> —Soren Kierkegaard

> "Everyone *has* a problem, *is* a prob-
> lem, or *lives* with one."
> —Sam Shoemaker

You want to change, to grow, to be fulfilled. What will it take to bring that about? In reality, the force is already there, awaiting your response and cooperation. Theologians call it the "prevenient grace of God," a term meaning that God always takes the initiative.

There is something within each of us which I call the "growth principle." It indwells every living thing. It throbs in every cell and vibrates in the pulsating atoms and neutrons and electrons which comprise each cell. It is the force which prompts a cell to divide, the principle which is responsible for ambition and aspiration, reverence and awe. It is the motivating power in every act of unselfishness and heroism. It is inherent in the conception, birth and growth of every infant. This creative drive is at work when two people fall in love and decide to spend the rest of their lives together.

Every seed that bursts forth into life and produces a plant is imbued with this mysterious force. This incredible power, crudely termed *instinct*, enables a bird, separated at birth from its mother, to build a nest identical with those built by its parents. There is no way to define this invincible, gentle, relentless force. And yet, we need to call it something for purposes of identification, even though the very name itself is limiting.

The mystical words with which John begins his gospel excite our wonder, but leave us breathless with a thousand questions: "When all things began, the Word already was. The Word dwelt with God, and what God was, the Word was. The Word, then, was with God at the beginning, and through him all things came to be; no single thing was created without him. All that came to be was alive with his life, and that life was the light of men." [1]

The Life Force Gives Impetus

This pulsating, creative Life Force, immutable and indescribable, energizes and gives impetus to every living thing and is one manifestation of God. John tells us that Jesus was the motivating factor in the creation of all things. Though we cannot understand this immanent, powerful, gentle, Life Force, it resides within each of us. It is life, aspiration, growth—in short, it is all that is creative and good. Among other things, it is the inner force which lures us toward a greater degree of wholeness.

If you aspire to *be* more, *love* more, *grow* more—if you are motivated to become whole and to be fulfilled—then this Life Force is at work within you. It appears to grow in intensity or to diminish, depending upon our degree of wholeness.

A man phoned me recently. He said his name was Jim Walker (his real name). He told me that he had joined a Yokefellow group in the McNeil Island penitentiary and had met me there some years ago when I spoke at the prison. I asked him to write me the details of his experience. He wrote a few days later after reaching his home in Billings, Montana, and sent me a color picture of himself in his place of business. He wrote:

Dear Dr. Osborne:
    It was nice talking to you the other day. I met you in 1962 while I was an inmate at McNeil Island. While there, the chaplain invited me to attend a Yokefellow group meeting. I didn't believe there was a God. God to me was something like Santa Claus—someone only kids and weaklings believe in. After listening to Larry Baulch speak (a former inmate of San Quentin, later an ordained minister and prison worker) and tell his life story, I felt a power stronger than I was. I began to take a real interest in my Yokefellow group and tried to find myself.

"I had been nothing but a troublemaker. . . . After three and a half years in the Yokefellow group I found God and myself. Before being in that group if I ever did anything for anyone else, I always wanted twice as much back. God is now using me to show others what he can do if they will let him.

"I have been to prison five times, a total of twenty years. I am now sixty-three years old and enjoying wonderful health. Most people take me for forty-five to fifty-five. The Federal judge who sent me to prison the last time has asked me to apply for a full pardon, for he has seen the change in me. I arrived in Billings, Montana, in 1967 with a prison-made suit and $7.50, no job and no place to live. My wife had divorced me while I was in prison and refused to let me see our two daughters.

"Finally I got a job at $2.00 an hour. In 1969 I remarried and started my own wholesale stereo business. I have a good business, with sales of $400,000 a year, belong to the Elks Club, and counsel men coming out of prison. I want my life to count for God. Pray for me.

Jim Walker

Twenty years is a long time to spend in prison. A chaplain's invitation and participation in a Yokefellow sharing group enabled Jim to start a whole new life. The Life Force was at work in him, and when he responded to the indwelling movement of this Force, the miracle took place.

Will Chemicals Solve Our Problems?

Psychologist Kenneth Clark, when he was inaugurated as president of the American Psychological Association, called for a new kind of chemical to deaden man's aggressiveness, and so make the world a less dangerous place. Freud once suggested that in order to change the world significantly one would have to get at the masses of men, and that the only way to accomplish this was through psychoanalysis. It is now known that fewer people get well as the result of psychoanalysis than through spontaneous remission (when nothing whatever is done for them). In his later years Freud came to see that the evil in the world is both inside man and outside of him, in nature, and so he became more pessimistic.

Men like psychologists Kenneth Clark and Sigmund Freud could not conceive of a significant change taking place in a person's life as the result of a conversion experience or as the result of someone mediating Christian love to another person. But it happens. Whether you call it the Word (Logos), Life Force, Christ, Holy Spirit or whatever, the fact remains that God has taken the initiative and waits only for your response. I do not want to make it sound simple, for it is not always easy. I have received hundreds of letters from desperately hurting people who have prayed and searched and agonized for years, trying to find a solution for their particular set of problems. One's heart goes out to them. The New Testament gives an account of a woman who had been making the rounds of the doctors for twelve years, without getting any help, before she touched the hem of Jesus' robe.[2] That's a long time to search for a cure.

How Long Will It Take?

I was counseling with a woman well past middle-age who was suffering from a depression so severe that at times she was suicidal. She also had a number of fairly serious physical complaints. A woman of above average intelligence, she had searched for years for the answer to her inner turmoil and physical disabilities. In the process of her Primal Integration therapy she kept asking plaintively, "Isn't there a quicker, easier way? How long is this going to take? It seems like I've been at this forever." It had actually been a matter of months, and already she could begin to see the improvement. She was no longer suicidal. Her depression was lifting. She was beginning to get her life somewhat in order; yet she continued to ask, "Isn't there a quicker way?"

My response was always the same: "How long did it take you to get this way? How long have you tried other methods without success?" She would reply, "Yes, I know. I'm getting better. But I want to be well *now*." So do we all.

Perhaps your prayers have echoed her desire for instant wholeness. This is understandable, for we humans suffer long, time is short, and growth toward wholeness is slow. Don't berate yourself for being impatient. It's normal to join the prophets of old, in the cry, "How long, O Lord, how long?"

Let's take a look at some of the factors which impede our growth. One of them is a largely unconscious resistance to change. Karl Menninger quotes Freud as saying that "the sufferer is always somewhat deterred by subversive, internal opposition to . . . the cure. He suffers on the one hand from the pains of his affliction and yearns to get well. But he suffers at the same time from traitorous impulses that fight against the accomplishment of any change in himself. . . . Like Hamlet he wonders whether it may be better after all to suffer the familiar pains and aches . . . than to face the complications of a new and strange (and) possibly better way of handling things." [3]

Having Realistic Goals

In the comic strip Peanuts, Charlie Brown and Linus are talking. Charlie says, "I hate to see the sun go down. I've wasted another day." Linus asks, "What do you consider a day not wasted?" Charlie Brown replies, "A day when I meet the girl of my dreams, am elected president of our country, have won the Nobel Prize, and have hit a home run."

Charles Schulz, the cartoonist—who, incidentally, is a devout Christian—is subtly pointing out the fallacy of unrealistic ambitions and our childhood love of instant gratification. There is a residual longing for quick solutions in most adults. Perhaps this desire for the instantaneous cure and the miraculous solution of our problems is the motivation which keeps us searching for better drugs, more effective methods, quicker modes of transportation and communication. The unrealistic dreams of childhood may well be a driving force behind man's search for the ultimate.

But meanwhile, until the one broad-spectrum drug to cure all ills has been discovered, and the quick-growth-toward-wholeness method perfected, we will have to utilize the means at hand.

Sadly enough, it is highly improbable that spiritual and emotional growth will ever be a quick or simple procedure. We have the same physical organism and emotional nature that Abraham had when he left Ur of the Chaldees and began his long journey. The same impulse which drove Cain to rise up and slay his brother Abel in the opening chapters of Genesis is still alive and functioning.

The key to growth seems to reside in motivation. And the two great motivators are pain—psychic, physical or situational—and the love of accomplishment. Dr. Hans Selye, discoverer of the stress theory underlying all disease, writes, "I am not going to tell you what should motivate you; whether you wish to serve God, King, Country, Family, Political Party, to work for good causes, or to fulfill your duty, is up to you. I only want to show that *motivation*—preferably an ambition to accomplish something that really satisfies you and hurts no one—is essential." [4]

Motivation Is Everything

So, what is your motivation? Are you suffering from emotional distress, physical pain, failure to find fulfillment, frustration over not achieving some significant goal, or impaired relationships? Whatever your difficulty, motivation is of paramount importance.

I recall from my childhood days a phrase used by an indolent farmer who spent most of his time sitting in front of the town's one store: "You know, I've got half a mind to do that." Since he had just half a mind to do it, his fences were down, his livestock untended, and his crops usually put in late. Half a mind is almost as bad as no mind at all. The Bible again and again stresses the importance of the "whole heart," "one heart" (singlemindedness) and "with all your heart." The emphasis here is upon singleness of purpose, the concentrating of one's forces upon a single goal.

Charlie Brown's goal of meeting the girl of his dreams, being elected president, winning the Nobel Prize, and hitting a home run is the very opposite of singlemindedness. There's nothing wrong with a person's longing to be prosperous, useful, happily married, fulfilled, to have lots of friends, a nice place in the country, to travel and perhaps go back to college and take a few courses. The difficulty is that each of these must be worked on *one at a time,* with single heartedness.

What Are Your Priorities?

There is the matter of establishing your priorities. I think of a greatly distraught woman with whom I was counseling, whose life was terribly disordered. She wanted release from her inner confusion and anxiety, and we worked on that. But I discovered that her life was so disorganized and her goals so unrealistic, that we had to begin by straightening out her priorities. She was a new Christian and desperately wanted to attend all of the Bible study classes and prayer groups available. She had a hopeless marriage and had instituted divorce proceedings, but her distractedness so confused her lawyer that he didn't get a court date. She needed an operation, but couldn't get around to setting a date for it. Relatives bombarded her with requests for emotional support, her estranged husband called her several times a day, and a dozen other claims on her time kept her so upset she couldn't think straight.

We began by setting priorities. She was to make this phone call today, another the next day, undertake project number three the following day, and so on, and report to me. The confusion was so great that it was four weeks before one important phone call was made. But one day she came in glowing. She had gotten four important things accomplished that day, and as a consequence her depression had lifted. She began to see that she could handle life *if she established priorities and undertook one thing at a time.*

What are your priorities? What is your most important need, or goal, at this moment? Instead of jumping to a quick conclusion, try writing down your current needs, as they come to mind. You can number them in the order of their importance later. One person came up with this list:

Financial and job security. (I'm not sure I am in the right job.)
Lessening of my anxiety. (I'm tense nearly all the time.)

Improving my marriage. (It's not bad, not good.)
See the doctor. (I have a troublesome symptom and can't find
  time to make an appointment with the doctor.)
Take a course on child-rearing. (Our kids are out of control.)
Get more exercise. (I'm getting flabby.)
Invite some friends in. (Social life is sagging badly.)
Sign up for the Bethel Bible class at church. (No time.)
Join a Yokefellow group. (If I can find a spare night.)
Get the back lawn reseeded.
Have the oil changed in my car.
Become a happier, less anxiety-ridden parent. (No patience with
  the kids.)
(There's more, but this is a start.)

Now, with a list like that—and it's not an unusual compilation
of goals and needs—one is likely to be confused and simply respond
to immediate crises and urgent demands. Before you read any
farther, I would urge you to sit down and make up your own
list, including not only major goals, but lesser needs as well, for
five or ten little ones can take as much energy as one big one. All
are important.

Now that your list is before you, put each item in one of these
four categories:

1. Urgent and imperative. Must be done at once.
2. Important, but can be undertaken days or weeks from now.
3. Can be delayed even longer without serious harm.
4. Put on the back burner indefinitely. No rush.

The person making the list given above finally decided that
having the oil changed in the car deserved a number one priority,
since an oil change was long overdue. Signing up for a course on
child-rearing was also a top priority item, since the children had
been getting out of hand, and neither parent knew precisely what
to do about it. (They subsequently learned in a night class at a
neighboring college that it wasn't so important what they did or
said to the kids, but it was imperative that they get themselves
straightened out, so they could be more patient and spend more
time with their children.) Priority was then given to signing up
for participation in a Yokefellow group in their church, since they
had learned that most group members gained a greater degree
of inner peace from such a sharing group.

Other priorities were given to the remaining items on the list.
Eventually they were all taken care of, *one at a time.*

List Your Goals! Be Specific!

If you have a welter of drives, aspirations, frustrations, goals and
needs, but do not have them written out, you will tend to suffer

from confusion and anxiey, not to mention frustration. Find out what is *most important in your life* and work on that with all your heart. If you discover yourself blocked momentarily in attaining some goal, set it aside for the time being, and select another item on your priority list. Often when we set a problem aside for a bit, new insight can be gained from the relinquishment of the item. One can then become more eligible for divine guidance than when facing a problem with intensity.

This brings us to the matter of divine guidance. First, let's look at the negative aspects, for guidance is not a simple matter. To illustrate my point: The church where I once served as a senior minister was searching for a director of Christian education. After a three month's search, the Board grew impatient and suggested appointing a committee to assist me. The committee went to work with great diligence. They first prayed for guidance, then confidently expected something good to happen. A day or so after they had prayed, the chairperson happened to be in a Christian bookstore and asked the manager if she knew of a good Christian education director. She replied, "Why, a young woman who just walked out the door asked me a minute or two ago if I knew of any openings for a Christian education worker." Our zealous committeewoman dashed out, found the young woman, and spent an hour with her discussing the job opening.

At a hastily called meeting of the committee it was announced that the "Lord has answered prayer, as he always does." The young woman so miraculously encountered seemed to be the right one for the job. The candidate met with the committee, impressed them greatly, and it was recommended, over my protest, that she be employed immediately. I was certain she did not have the background or qualifications we needed.

But the Board, eager to get on with the project, voted to employ her. She went to work with great diligence, first organizing our church library. That took her three months, during which time she did nothing else. When asked to undertake some youth activities she seemed bewildered, and after six months of inept performance she resigned to take up missionary work in Nigeria.

Divine Guidance and Wishful Thinking

A good friend of mine, a prominent businessman, full of the zeal of the recent convert, was asked to try to find an outstanding speaker for a men's brotherhood dinner at their church. He learned that Jimmy Carter, then a presidential candidate, was to speak at a men's banquet in a nearby city. My friend prayed earnestly and at great length about this and finally "received the as-

surance" that Jimmy Carter was their man. Accordingly, he drove
to the neighboring city to attend the banquet in the hope of
meeting Mr. Carter and issuing the invitation.

As he entered the banquet hall he was met by an old friend
who said, "Vince! Great to see you! What are you doing here?
Say, I'm looking for someone to give the invocation. We're late
now. Come on up to the speaker's table and do this for us." Vince
was gratified, for now he knew divine guidance was operating,
and when he was seated next to Jimmy Carter, the conviction
deepened.

During the dinner he chatted with Mr. Carter, and finally invited him to be the speaker at the forthcoming dinner at their
church. Mr. Carter said he would be delighted to accept if that
date was open and would write him as soon as he could check
his appointment calendar. Vince was thrilled.

A few days later the letter came. He opened it with confident
expectation. It was brief. Mr. Carter was scheduled to speak elsewhere on that date, and couldn't possibly accede to the request,
much as he would like to. Vince smiled ruefully as he told me
of his gradually growing awareness that coincidence, high hopes,
expectation and wishful thinking are easily confused with divine
guidance.

Prayer and a Financial Fiasco

When I was much younger, I once prayed earnestly about a
rather important investment I was contemplating. I genuinely
wanted guidance, for I didn't want to make a mistake. Looking
back I can see that I so desperately wanted to make the investment
that wishful thinking clouded both my judgment and affected my
prayers adversely. The partnership needed considerably more
money than I had available and so, having heard of "open and
closed doors," I prayed that if I should make the investment, the
additional funds would be forthcoming. I had no inkling as to
where the money might come from.

In a few days, to my immense surprise, the precise amount
of money fell into my hands, and I plunged. Well, that investment
was a disaster. Not only did I lose my entire investment, but I
had to put up additional funds in a futile effort to save the
original investment. Besides, it took a vast amount of time which
I could ill afford to spend. I was younger, then, and have since
learned that there are no simplistic rules governing divine guidance.

I learned then, and subsequently, that there are several basic
principles involved. First of all, God is not waiting for us to
seek guidance. He is broadcasting it 24 hours a day, 365 days a

year. He always takes the initiative. I need not beg or beseech, or bargain, with God. All that is necessary is that I *get my inner life in order and learn to listen.* This is not easy. It requires discipline. It's harder for many people to sit and be quiet for an hour than it is to go out and pull up weeds for half a day.

And second, one must want God's will, not only in a crisis but *in every area of life.* I cannot have his will in this matter if I do not want it in that. There is a seldom understood scripture which touches on this fact in an interesting way. Jesus said, "Whoever has the will to do the will of God shall know. . . . " [5] There is much more to that statement, but even that much of it contains a great truth, which is that one who *wants* the will of God will know the truth. Such a one will know inwardly, with a growing certainty, how to separate wishful thinking and coincidence from God's will.

Do you want the whole will of God in your life, all of the time, in every area? You may not be *doing* the will of God all of the time; most people aren't, for we are all marred. But one who earnestly *desires* the will of God in every area of life can *know.*

Not wanting the will of God can stem from blatant rebellion or from a distorted concept of God's will. God desires your best. He wants you to experience love, joy, peace, and fulfillment. The fear that if you sought his full will in your life he might deny you something worthwhile or send you to Outer Mongolia as a missionary is a mistaken concept. Some people, reared in a grim, joyless religious environment, often have an understandable reluctance to submit completely to God's will.

God Will Guide But Not Control You

Others fear that God will take over their wills. Far from it! In fact, this is one thing God will not do. He refuses to coerce us. The problem is, not that he will force us into something undesirable, but that we have so much freedom we don't always know how to handle it wisely.

I have mentioned two requirements for discovering God's will. The first is to learn to be quiet and receptive, not just on the one day you desire guidance, but consistently; the second is to *want* God's will; and the third is to utilize the God-given intelligence available to us. For instance, if before I had made my disastrous investment I had consulted with several friends who were more knowledgeable in the field than I, the mistake could have been avoided. Though I did not have an adequate background and expertise, there were friends and acquaintances who did. There is the classic story of the little old lady who lodged with the Better Business Bureau a complaint against a fraudulent investment scheme. They asked her why she had not consulted them before she made the investment. She said, "I was afraid you'd tell me not to do it." That had been my problem.

There are innumerable stories of people who, in a sudden crisis, have prayed with remarkable results. Like the gamblers who tell with glee of their winnings, but seldom speak of their losses, we have a tendency to repeat the occasional miraculous prayer results and ignore the many prayer requests which were not granted for a number of good reasons.

In general it can be said that one who prays in a panic, while his prayer *may* be answered, stands a far better chance if he has been praying all along. Not that God rejects the once-in-a-while pray-er. It is just that one who plays golf or tennis once a year will play less well than someone who plays regularly. We feel more confidence if we have been "practicing"—whether it be a sport, music, or our religion.

One needs to "practice the presence of God," so that it seems natural and instinctive. Consider the difference of a person who approaches God and says, "Lord, I haven't been around for a long time. In fact I haven't even been attending church. Praying seems rather strange, because I've been a stranger to it for so long. But I'm in a jam and need help. Now, here's the problem. . . . " Depending on many factors—faith, urgency, humility, validity of the request—the request may or may not be granted. But it is safe to say that the occasional, only-in-a-jam pray-er is far less likely to be effective in his petition. "You will seek the Lord your God, and you will find him, *if you search after him with all your heart and with all your soul*." [6] (Author's italics.)

The Door in the Wall

H.G. Wells once wrote a fascinating story called "The Door in the Wall." It deals with a man who finally achieved great success and considerable acclaim who, as a small child, found his way through a door into a magnificently beautiful garden. While there, he was in another world. It was infinitely satisfying. Walking about in the garden he felt a sense of deep peace and serenity. Then he had to leave.

From time to time he tried to find the door in the wall again, but never succeeded. On six or more subsequent occasions, however, as a grown man, he glimpsed the tiny door to the mystical garden, but in each instance he had pressing engagements and did not have the time to enter it.

The second time he saw the door he was on his way to take

the final exams which would lead to an Oxford career. On a third occasion others were observing, and he was deterred by what they might think if he stopped to enter the mysterious garden. Another day he passed up the opportunity because of an urgent matter in which his honor was involved, and he could not take the time. On the next two occasions there were pressing personal and professional demands which prevented him from going through the garden door: he was on his way to an imperative vote in the House of Commons, and the other time he was hurrying to visit his dying father. A final opportunity was passed up because he had a chance to become a cabinet minister.

The things which deterred him were worthwhile, or at least understandable; but in each case the good became the enemy of the best. We are always free to pass by the little door that leads to emotional growth, to spiritual fulfillment, peace of mind, and serenity. But no good thing ever comes *unless we sacrifice some lesser good.*

Paths to Wholeness

In the next chapters are described some doors which may offer you entry into another dimension of spiritual and emotional wholeness. Your choice of a doorway may be different from that of someone else, for we are at different points in our journey, with varying needs and preferences. It is important that you try, with all your heart, to discover the door which will lead you to a greater degree of wholeness.

Someone has said that when you can't get a piece of equipment assembled properly, always look in the waste basket for the discarded instructions and read them carefully. Most humans approach life as if there were no instructions available, or necessary. When difficulties arise they seem puzzled or hurt. If they are wise they will begin looking for the instructions. These are largely contained in the Bible and elaborated upon by thousands of writers who have taken great biblical principles and run them through the fine mesh of their own experience.

One or more of the methods and principles enunciated in the next chapters can lead you to wholeness and growth as they have many thousands of other people.

13

Paths to Wholeness

"I'm trying to grow up before I crack up."
—Remark by a member of a Yokefellow group

In these last two chapters, I want to share with you various means and methods leading to wholeness. I happen to be familiar with a number of these particular approaches and movements and have had an opportunity to evaluate some of their results.

Psychiatry

Several years ago I was asked by the San Mateo County Mental Health Associations, consisting of psychiatrists, psychologists, ministers, and social workers, to speak at their luncheon meeting, and to describe our Yokefellow movement, with particular reference to the spiritual growth inventories which we use. These are standardized psychological tests adapted to emotional and spiritual growth, using a bi-weekly feedback system of evaluation slips. They are used by the group members during the sessions to point up areas of the personality in need of attention.

I spoke to the group for a hour and was invited to speak again at the next meeting a month later. The response was positive, except for the reaction of a psychiatrist who said to me after the meeting: "I think you should get a foundation grant and make a study to determine how much damage you people are doing."

"Fine," I replied, "but let's get a larger foundation grant and make a study at the same time to see how much damage you psychiatrists are doing." I smiled, but he didn't.

"That's already been done," he said.

"What were the findings?"

There was a brief pause, rather a pained one I felt.

"Well, they studied two hundred schizophrenics in Los Angeles

158

County. One hundred of them got standard psychiatric treatment, and the others received no psychotherapy of any kind. They found that precisely as many of the *untreated* schizophrenics recovered as those who received psychiatric treatment."

"So?"

"Well," he replied with a sigh, "we just go on doing the best we can."

Psychiatrist H. J. Eysenck has presented significant statistical evidence indicating that psychotherapy *on the average* achieves no better results than are realized by spontaneous remission. (Recovery which takes place simply with the passing of time.)

Another researcher, Dr. Jerome Frank,[1] found that about two-thirds of the patients seeing a psychotherapist showed improvement, but the same proportion of untreated patients also seemed to recover. A substantial number of other studies have reported approximately the same findings.

One research group compared recovery rates of mental hospital patients receiving group therapy with the recovery rates of patients involved in drama group activity. They found a greater improvement rate in the drama group patients.

"Furthermore, on the basis of studies by Levitt (1957), Eysenck (1960), Mink and Isaacson (1959), and others, the evidence now available suggests that on the average, psychotherapy may be harmful as often as helpful, with an average effect comparable to receiving no help." [2]

The "UPC" Factor

As was to be expected, studies of the relative effectiveness of a group of psychiatrists revealed that some achieved excellent results, while others did not. A study undertaken by Whiteborn and Betz of Johns Hopkins University, compared seven well-functioning psychiatrists whose schizophrenic patient improvement was 75 percent with seven poorly-rated psychiatrists with similar training whose improvement rate was only 27 percent. There is abundant evidence that it is not the training, or psychiatric orientation, which makes the difference in a therapist, *but his or her personality and attitude*. This in no way minimizes the value of training, but does stress the overwhelming importance of the UPC factor— Unconditional Positive Caring.

I have related elsewhere the incident told to me by a psychiatrist at the Camarillo State Hospital in California. He stated that they had seventy-six therapy groups meeting weekly, but they had run out of leaders, and there was no one to convene one group. Someone suggested that the only staff member not leading a group was the truck driver. In desperation he was permitted to convene the group, but was watched carefully to make certain he made no serious errors. At the end of the first year it was discovered that more of his group members had left the hospital, and a smaller percentage had returned, than from any other group. My informant said, "I was then appointed by the staff to study him and see how he did it. I found three things: he used basic common sense, he genuinely cared about those people, and he was strong and took no foolishness from them."

I am currently involved with a man of fifty, an engineer, who has been seeing psychiatrists off and on for thirty years. He is in no sense an emotional basket case, for he functions normally in a highly technical field and is quite successful in most of his relationships. However, he has been searching for the roots of his excess anxiety, which produces undue tension, and makes him less effective than he desires to be.

Diagnosis and Insight Do Not Guarantee Recovery

For twelve years he saw a highly competent psychiatrist two to three times a week. He feels he derived considerable insight and is grateful for that. However, he reports that his anxiety did not lessen in the slightest. This is understandable, for it is a well-established fact that *insight seldom cures*. The knowledge that I have a tumor does not remove it. Diagnosis does not constitute recovery.

Despite what may sound like a negative note concerning psychiatry, it needs to be said that at the Burlingame Counseling Center [3] we sometimes make referrals to psychiatrists. This is especially true when the counselee shows psychotic tendencies or is in need of medication.

On behalf of psychiatry it should be pointed out that there are many unknowns. There are cases of severe depression, for instance, for which no permanent cure has been found. Often the cause is unknown, and frequently medication does not help. There is no known cure for schizophrenia, which is actually a catch-all term covering a whole galaxy of symptoms. Psychology is much more of an art than an exact science, and there is much to learn about the cause and cure of mental illness.

Group Therapy

In the last twenty years there has been a proliferation of therapy groups bearing many different names, and with a wide variety of methodology. Some have flourished for a time and vanished. Others, with methods and techniques which have produced better results, are still functioning.

In hundreds of mental health facilities therapy groups meet weekly or oftener for sharing. It is a vital and productive adjunct to whatever other type of treatment the patients may be receiving.

In our culture much communication tends to deal with either gossip or trivia. Our relationships are usually rather superficial. Friends who have known each other for five or twenty years seldom know what the other feels at a deep level. In most therapy groups a "climate" is established which encourages the sharing of feelings. In some types of groups there are few if any ground rules. Others stress certain basic guidelines, such as the requirement to deal with feelings rather than concepts. Usually advice is discouraged, but this is not true of all.

Some therapy groups encourage confrontation and attack. For some types of persons this approach seems to work, especially with some drug addicts and alcoholics. The chief benefit derived from the attack method is that one's defenses are shattered. Those who have a strong defense system, and who insist on rationalizing their neurotic conduct, often require such an approach. Others, with a less rigid personality and defense system, avoid such groups like the plague, and in most instances should. Few people enjoy having their masks ripped away in a sudden attack by fellow group members. A much gentler, gradual approach seems indicated for most people.

Virtually every city and most smaller towns have therapy groups of some kind. Most Mental Health facilities offer such techniques.

There are other groups which stand midway between therapy and spiritual growth. This area is not easy to define. For instance, most churches offer Bible study and prayer groups. Some of these, of course, are more effective than others, but in general it can be said that the accumulation of Bible verses may not have any significant effect upon one's growth toward wholeness. Intellectual knowledge alone, good as it is, can produce few results in terms of changed personality or life situation. (This fact is dealt with in more depth in the section devoted to Yokefellow groups.)

TA (Transactional Analysis)

Eric Berne, author of *Games People Play*, was intrigued at how quickly many of his patients seemed to change in facial expression, body language, and vocabulary. To quote Thomas Harris, who has carried on Berne's work: "A thirty-five-year-old lawyer whom [Berne] was treating said, 'I'm not really a lawyer, I'm just a little boy.' Away from the psychiatrist's office he was, in fact, a successful lawyer, but in treatment he felt and acted like a little boy. Sometimes during the hour he would ask, 'Are you talking to the lawyer or to the little boy?' Both Berne and his patient became intrigued at the existence and appearance of these two real people, or states of being, and began talking about them as 'the adult' and 'the child.' Treatment concentrated around separating the two. Later another state began to become apparent, distinct from 'adult' and 'child.' This was 'the parent,' and was identified by behavior which was a reproduction of what the patient saw and heard his parents do when he was a little boy." [4]

The Three Ego States

A basic concept of TA revolves around the need to identify these three "ego states" or states of being. With a little patience and insight one can discover these. A forty-year-old woman told me that when she visited her parents she felt about eight years old. A single sentence from her mother, a gesture, or a particular tone of voice, made her feel instantly like a child. "During my entire visit I am their child and act that way. In another part of my mind I am seething with rage, just as I did as a child when my controlling mother made a compliant little zombie out of me. Then, when I come home and find my own kids out of control I catch myself screaming at them. A bit later when I quiet down I tell my husband calmly all about it. I am aware of those three states—child with my mother, screaming parent with my children, and an adult with my husband."

This concept is relatively easy to understand, especially when we see it operating in others. TA, however, involves more than a simple understanding of the three states of being. There is a fairly complex interaction between any two or more people involving specialized TA terminology, and the various games people play.

I encourage counselees to read, *I'm OK–You're OK*,[5] and to learn to identify the ego states always operating in our personalities. There are TA workshops and seminars conducted in many parts of the United States. In fact, it is probably one of the most widely known of all the various therapies. Most people could profit from reading the book and from participating in a TA seminar or group.

Having said that most people could benefit from an exposure to TA principles, it must also be said that the mere understanding of these concepts does not constitute a cure for deeply rooted personality problems, any more than a course in New Testament Christianity will necessarily make one a Christian. However, TA terminology has so thoroughly entered the vocabulary of millions of people that it forms a basis for communication as well as understanding human interaction.

TA terminology can be used in virtually any other type of

therapy, for it is fundamental to an understanding of the way we change our emotional states without conscious thought or intent.

The Institutional Church

They were having a quarrel in the church at Corinth. In the opening chapters of his first letter to the church, the Apostle Paul mentions a whole galaxy of arguments which raged among the members. He refers to dissension, quarreling, jealousy, strife, pride, arrogance, immorality, boasting, law suits between fellow members, and in addition, the church was split four ways. Some claimed to be the followers of Paul, some of Apollos, others of Cephas, while another group insisted they were followers of Christ. Then, too, they had a major division over spiritual gifts. One group felt that the "gift of tongues" was of supreme importance; others disputed this.

The church has been marred by dissension and excesses ranging from violent theological quarrels, to the burning of dissidents at the stake. It is not a pretty picture. I recall hearing, as a child, passionate debates between proponents of various denominations concerning moot points of theology. People took their church doctrine so seriously in those days that, while they did not burn each other at the stake for alleged heresy, they did burn with righteous indignation over the theological errors of their neighbors. In these days of church unity and ecumenicity the idea of such debates and angry religious confrontation brings only amused, tolerant smiles.

Generalizations are always suspect. One cannot say of the institutional church that it is this or that. Having conducted weekend seminars in something over a hundred different churches of a dozen major denominations, I can testify to the fact that the Christian church is alive and well. Its condition ranges from good to magnificent. I have spoken in churches with memberships of two hundred to nine thousand, and I've found in most of them an amazing warmth and vitality and love.

Not everyone has had a happy church experience. My childhood was both blessed and marred by the churches I attended. They were the product of their time and culture, and some presented the gospel in frightening, condemnatory, legalistic tones. As a result, I grew up with a monumental guilt complex which lasted for years. However, I seldom left a service without a generalized feeling that I wanted to be a better person.

The Church Is Divine in Origin

The Christian church, marred as it has been by the excesses of

its leaders, and frailties of its members, is the only divine institution on earth: "On this rock I will build my church, and the
forces of death shall never overpower it." [6] For all its weaknesses,
it is our best and finest hope.

Most denominations today are marked not so much by important
doctrinal distinctions as by differences in emphasis, liturgy, and
the type of activities they offer their members. A noted psychologist
has stated that there is more therapy being offered Sunday morning in the churches than anywhere else in America.

I would urge you to identify yourself with a local church if you
are not already a member. If your experience has led you to believe
that contemporary churches are irrelevant, boring, and stodgy, I
suggest that you shop around more widely. There are so many
different kinds of churches and emphases that ultimately you are
almost certain to find one which fits your needs. Denominational
lines have become blurred. One may occasionally find a Methodist
or Baptist church with a formal service, and a Catholic church
with an informal, contemporary worship service. Many churches
offer a traditional worship service at 11:00 A.M., and a more informal, contemporary one at an earlier hour. The churches of
today, except in some smaller communities where there may be
little variety, offer a veritable cafeteria of choices. Don't let some
ancient childhood impressions sour you on the church. It has
changed—in most instances.

And ministerial training has changed. Many ministers today
have had clinical training and quite often are competent counselors.
While there are still ministers who are dealing with dead issues,
answering questions no one is asking any more, a majority of
contemporary pastors are dealing with current issues and problems.

The Church of Jesus Christ, whose divine origin is attested
to by its continued existence for two thousand years, despite the
failures of its members, is still the greatest power for good in this
world of dubious values. Its weaknesses and excesses have been no
greater than those of science or education, for instance, whose
blunders are simply those of faulty human beings.

The Acid Test

A woman told me that she had been astounded by the lack of
love and understanding shown by her minister in dealing with a
young woman undergoing a stressful situation. "I was raised in
that church," she said. "I don't want to leave it. It's *my* church,
but I can't listen to a man preach who shows so little love. What
can I do?"

"Apply the acid test of Christianity," I replied.

"What's that?"

"Jesus said, 'by this all men will know that you are my disciples, if you have love for one another.' [7] Find a church where you can sense that kind of love among the members, and in the minister. Don't let false loyalty to childhood memories keep you tied to a church that is legalistic rather than loving." In seeking a church home, most people today are searching for relationships, warmth, love and concern, rather than theological minutiae.

The Charismatic Movement

The "tongues" or charismatic movement, as most participants prefer to call it, is a rather controversial but rapidly growing activity which was a unique aspect of the Pentecostal churches until recent years. It has now spread across denominational lines and has touched both ministers and members of most major denominations.

The charismatic experience is loosely defined as "ecstatic utterance, usually unintelligible, accompanying religious excitation; the charismatic gift of ecstatic speech." [8]

The "gift of tongues," dealt with in the 12th, 13th, and 14th chapters of First Corinthians, refers to the gift of an unintelligible language normally used in private devotions, but also employed at times in worship services. Apparently this gift had gotten out of hand in the church at Corinth, for Paul writes, "I thank God that I speak in tongues more than you all; nevertheless, in church I would rather speak five words with my mind, in order to instruct others, than ten thousand words in a tongue." [9] He encourages them to continue with their ecstatic speaking [10] but insists that when it is done in a church service there must be someone who can interpret what is said.[11]

I have known individuals of various denominations who "received the gift" who were warm, loving, joyous Christians. I have also met others with the same gift who were contentious and quarrelsome. One is led to the conclusion that the gift of tongues is not necessarily a personality changing experience, that it does not always improve one's disposition, but that for many Christians it is an added dimension of genuine significance. Those in the charismatic movement tend to be enthusiastic, happy individuals. On the negative side, some charismatics, whom I have dealt with in counseling, had been assured that this gift was going to rid them forever of their depression, or neurosis, or other personality hangups. In some instances there was an initial upswing out of depression, a temporary lifting of some ancient burden, followed by a subsequent let-down. Others with whom I have dealt seemed to have derived significant permanent benefits, both from the gift of tongues—used in private prayer—and from the warm, loving fellowship usually found in the charismatic fellowship.

Rev. Dennis Bennett, an Episcopal priest ministering to a dynamic church, has written that "the passages in several modern versions of the Scripture that speak of 'tongues of ecstasy,' or 'ecstatic speech' are paraphrases rather than translations. There is nothing in the Greek original to imply that speaking in tongues had anything to do with excitement, ecstasy, frenzy, etc. The phrase is always just *lalein glossais,* meaning simply 'to speak in languages.'

"Speaking in tongues may stir the emotions, just as it may sharpen the intellect, and order the will, and we hope it does these things; but you do not have to become emotional in order to speak in tongues. As a matter of fact, one of the greatest blocks to the receiving of the Holy Spirit is the highly charged emotional atmosphere that is thought by some to be helpful or even necessary. When people are seeking to receive the baptism of the Holy Spirit and speak in tongues for the first time, we try to keep their emotions as 'calm' as possible. Many begin to speak in tongues rather quietly. Later they will speak more strongly as faith grows and fear is overcome. Actually, excited emotions get in the way of the Holy Spirit just as much as an overactive intellect or an over-determined will!" [12]

I have known occasional instances where the charismatic issue has seemed divisive; but when it is handled properly there need not be contentiousness. A minister who exhibited great wisdom and love told me that his church could have been split over the charismatic issue, but he urged understanding, love, and tolerance on the part of the members, with the result that all tension vanished. It is seldom an issue that causes divisiveness, but littleness of spirit, and an absence of Christian love.

Retreats

The retreat movement has gained considerable impetus in recent years. In the San Francisco Bay Area where I live, there are a score of retreat centers, ranging from simple rustic mountain accommodations to more elaborate and comfortable facilities. Roman Catholics, in many areas, have led the way, particularly with their Marriage Enrichment Retreats. These are usually open to the general public, and participants give enthusiastic reports.

Retreats are valuable, however, an *annual* retreat seldom provides both a life-changing and growth-sustaining impetus. A weekend experience once a year can prove enormously helpful, and I encourage this enthusiastically; but it needs to be followed up by participation in an on-going fellowship or the results of the retreat diminish very rapidly. The founder of Esalen, a nationally known and somewhat controversial retreat center in Northern California, reported that 95 percent of their retreat participants indicated significant gains at the end of their stay, but a year later precisely the same percentage reported no permanent benefit. It seems naïve to expect a single weekend experience to enrich one's life permanently without the continued support and stimulation provided by a Christian fellowship or support group.

Jesus took his disciples on an extended retreat,[13] and most Christians can profit from the rest, stimulation, and inspiration provided by an occasional retreat, particularly if they are regular participants in a Christian fellowship.

14

More Paths to Wholeness

> "Our normal waking consciousness . . .
> is but one special type . . . whilst all
> about it, parted by the filmiest of
> screens, there lie potential forms of
> consciousness entirely different."
> —William James

Someone quipped that the nice thing about meditation is that it makes doing nothing quite respectable. However, meditation is not doing nothing, as it might appear to an onlooker. Sitting in one position for twenty minutes twice a day, trying to still the turbulent mind and focus on a single word or thought is *work*. It requires discipline; but it is one of the most rewarding paths to wholeness. Let's look at some of the various forms of meditation, and then review some of its limitations.

Forms of Meditation

We of the Western world are frantic activitists. With our instant coffee, rapid transit, quick food chains, and jet travel, we are somewhat like the harrassed man who mounted his horse, booted and spurred, and rode off in all directions. The tangible results are apparent in the form of our lush culture and enormous prosperity. But some of the side effects are manifest in the vast incidence of excessive anxiety, mental illness, and an oppressive aimlessness. "Where do I go from here? What is life all about? What is the source of my diffused anxiety and tension? Who am I?"

As if in answer to the Western world's frenzy and growing discontent, late in the 1950s a diminutive missionary named Mararish Mahesh Yogi came from the East to proclaim the virtues of what has come to be called TM (Transcendental Meditation). It is an outgrowth of the mystical Advaita school of Yoga and uses a Vedic devotional as an initiation rite. Though its founder claims it is not a religion, his writings and messages are sprinkled with Sanskrit phrases. Most of the practitioners of TM insist that there are no religious connotations involved.

Nearly 30,000 persons a month sign up for the course of instruction at a current fee of $125.00. There are TM centers throughout the country. Stanford University law professor John Kaplan describes it as a "non-chemical tranquilizer with no unpleasant side effects." Thousands of men and women from all walks of life have claimed benefit from TM.

An occasional negative note is heard. One zealous meditator decided that "more is better," and began to meditate up to eight hours a day, whereupon he became psychotic. He claimed that this form of meditation opened him up to demonic forces which took over his mind. It is my considered opinion that one who attempts to increase the suggested dosage of anything by ten times is probably a borderline psychotic to begin with.

I am not an ardent proponent of TM, particularly in view of the fact that recent studies have shown that it is not necessary to pay $125.00 to learn how to meditate. In *The Relaxation Response*,[1] Dr. Herbert Benson, associate professor of medicine at the Harvard Medical School, has shown that it is not necessary to undertake special training in order to learn how to meditate; nor is it important to receive the mysterious mantra (a word repeated silently and repetiously) given to each TM "graduate."

As the result of extensive studies of practitioners of TM and other forms of meditation, Dr. Benson reports that "tests at the Thorndike Memorial Laboratory have shown that a similar technique used with any sound or phrase or prayer or mantra brings forth the same (emotional and physical) changes noted during Transcendental Meditation." Among the reported results of continued meditation are lowered blood pressure, decreased anxiety and tension, a greater sense of inner peace and serenity, and greater effectiveness in daily living.

Dr. Benson names six important aspects of his form of meditation, which he calls "the Relaxation Response":

1. Sit quietly in a comfortable position.
2. Close your eyes.
3. Deeply relax all of your muscles, beginning at your feet and progressing up to your face. Keep them relaxed.
4. Breathe through your nose. Become aware of your breathing. As you breathe out, say the word "one", silently or to yourself.
5. Continue for ten to twenty minutes. You may open your eyes

to check the time, but do not use an alarm. When you finish, sit quietly for several minutes, at first with your eyes closed and later with eyes opened. Do not stand up for a few minutes.

6. Do not worry about whether you are successful in achieving a deep level of relaxation. Maintain a passive attitude and permit relaxation to occur at its own pace. When distracting thoughts intrude, try to ignore them by not dwelling upon them, and return to repeating "one." Practice the technique once or preferably twice a day, but not within two hours after any meal, since the digestive precess seems to interfere with the Relaxation Response.

Release from Physical Symptoms

Many people who suffer anxiety attacks, hypertension, and a number of other physical symptoms, report improvement after attempting this method of relaxation and meditation. Benson and others say, however, that some people who meditate several hours a day for weeks at a time tend to hallucinate, but no one has observed ill effects from two twenty minute periods a day of meditation.

Greedy seekers after quick cures will probably derive little if any benefit from any form of meditation. To be effective it must be done on a regular basis and over an extended period.

Studies have shown that meditators whose high blood pressure dropped to normal ranges found that when they stopped meditating their blood pressure rose again. The same is true of anxiety or any other symptom; for meditation is not a permanent "cure." It relieves but does not resolve the underlying cause of anxiety and tension.

An ancient mystic, Lao Tse, has expressed it well: "Muddy water, let stand, becomes clear." Most people find their minds cluttered with minutiae which, while of little importance, must be taken care of. Life is tension-producing. Relationships are often strained. In addition to current life problems which produce anxiety, there are anywhere from scores to hundreds of anxiety-producers buried in the unconscious mind. These are the unresolved fears and hurts of childhood which, while they originated in the past, are operating in the present to produce anxiety. This will be dealt with later in the material concerning Primal Integration.

A woman in her fifties told me during a counseling session, of her wide assortment of paralyzing phobias. Most of them, I found, were displaced fears originating in her childhood. She had attended a judgmental, legalistic, condemnatory type of church as a child, and in fact still belonged to the same denomination. Her religious background had taken its toll. She knew intellectually that God loved her, but emotionally she felt condemned. One Sunday the pastor urged everyone in the congregation to spend ten minutes daily in silence, listening to what God was saying to them. She was among those who consented. The first day, she said, she closed her eyes for the period of silence with some trepidation. "I was sure God was going to judge me for my lack of faith. If I only had enough faith I wouldn't have all these stupid fears. But in just a few minutes, as I got quiet and erased all thoughts from my mind, I heard an inner voice saying, very distinctly, 'I love you, June.'"

Most of our troubles have come upon us because we will not spend ten to twenty minutes morning and night in silent meditation. Most people would prefer to wash dishes, dig in the garden, or clean out the garage, than to spend those few minutes in quiet meditation. All our protestations are neurotic rationalizations. The truth is that we are doing at any given time the thing we prefer to do, considering the alternatives. When you are hurting enough, desperate enough, perhaps you will begin to discipline yourself to do that most difficult of all things—sit in silence and learn to listen to what God is saying to you.

Faith at Work

One dynamic approach to spiritual growth is the Faith at Work movement. Originating in the Calvary Episcopal Church of New York City some fifty years ago under the leadership of Sam Shoemaker, this movement has become a non-denominational movement reaching tens of thousands of people.

Walden Howard, Director of Publications and Editor of Faith/At/Work tells of his first encounter with the group:

> My wife and I were invited to a small informal meeting in an engineer's home where we were encouraged to introduce ourselves 'more than skin deep.' I heard Christians for the first time in my life letting their hair down, admitting to their struggles and doubts while at the same time they shared their joy and faith. I found it both intriguing and scary. But that night as Esther and I left the meeting we turned to each other and said simultaneously, 'These are our people.'
>
> As we began to meet week after week with this group of very human Christians we began to discover that God makes himself known to us not only on the vertical level in answer to prayer or through the reading of the Bible, but on the horizontal through others of his own people.

The field ministry department of Faith at Work keeps in touch with groups of people in many states who wish to band together to discover how they can provide resources for churches in their areas. Hundreds of people come together for weekend experiences to attend workshops and wrestle with the implications of the gospel in their lives. Leadership training institutes limited to sixty persons are conducted at various points throughout the country for a period of six days. Another department of the organization publishes the Faith/At/Work magazine eight times a year. It reaches a paid subscriber circulation of forty thousand people and is an outstanding, vital, stimulating magazine. Additional information concerning the organization and its ministry can be secured by writing to Faith At Work, 111065 Little Patuxent Parkway, Columbia, Maryland, 21044. A number of Protestant denominations have organized similar programs under varying names: Lay Witness Mission, among the Methodists; The Macedonia Ministry served the American Baptists; and Faith Alive is the name under which Episcopalians conduct a similar program.

Institute of Church Renewal

The Institute of Church Renewal, with headquarters at 1870 Tucker Industrial Road, Tucker, Georgia, 30084, has as its chief purpose "the creation and distribution of resources to strengthen the local church and make faith more meaningful for the people of God." They have provided materials for churches of thirty-two denominations. Ben Johnson is the dynamic founder and president of the organization.

Yokefellow Groups

The Yokefellow movement originally had as its chief goal the formation of small fellowship groups within the framework of the local church. The emphasis of Yokefellows International is currently on institutes and retreat centers. There are a number of such centers in various parts of the country, the addresses of which can be obtained by writing to Yokefellows International, 920 Earlham Drive, Richmond, Indiana, 47374.

Yokefellows, Inc. (19 Park Road, Burlingame, California, 94010), founded in 1957, continues to be devoted to the principle of the small group and has been instrumental in helping to establish several thousand groups in all fifty states and ten foreign countries.

Based upon the concept that barriers to spiritual growth must be identified before they can be removed, Yokefellows, Inc. provides basic materials to enable groups to function successfully. Leadership is usually provided by a minister, though many groups have been successfully led by lay persons. One basic ingredient is the

Spiritual Growth Inventory consisting of standardized psychological tests adapted to spiritual and emotional growth. The purpose of these is to assist the participants in discovering barriers to personal growth. The individuals comprising the group, numbering eight to twelve, receive bi-weekly evaluation slips which they deal with in the weekly meetings. The slips point up gently, but insightfully, certain areas of the personality in need of attention. Each person receives a total of eleven or more such slips during a twenty-two week period. Some seventy thousand persons have participated in such groups.

One aspect of a properly conducted group is the loving acceptance generated. Most people have some difficulty in accepting themselves fully, and the group process creates a feeling of love and understanding which is spiritually and emotionally very healing. One woman writes:

> The group experience was the best thing that ever happened to me. I have never had so many people love me. I found it to be a great spiritual gain. During my Quiet Time life took on a new meaning. I have been told that I have changed greatly, all for the better. The people in the group have become very meaningful to me.

Another group member wrote:

> I thought the Spiritual Growth Inventory was rather dumb when I took it, but I later realized it was great! And the love and support of the group members were like nothing I have ever experienced. I would certainly recommend this experience to everyone. I don't want the group to end. The love and joy and growth have been more than I expected, and my relationships will never be the same.

Primal Integration

Far more effective for many persons than psychiatry, psychoanalysis, or any other form of "talk therapy" is a new approach called Primal Integration. It is similar in some ways to The Healing of Memories, though far more intensive. Arthur Janov, author of *The Primal Scream*,[2] *The Primal Revolution*,[3] and other books, was one of several persons who some years ago discovered the basic principle more or less simultaneously. The primal approach goes far deeper than traditional types of therapy. In the hands of a *thoroughly competent therapist* it produces remarkable results.

A lovely young married woman finally got up enough courage to confer with her pastor about some serious personal problems. She was a Sunday school teacher, sang in the choir, and had a good marriage; but, for some reason that she could not understand, she was somewhat sexually permissive, and her drinking pattern was such that she feared she was becoming an alcoholic. Her pastor, though a very competent counselor, found that she needed something more than confession and talk therapy. She seemed driven compulsively to do things she didn't want to do, which made no sense at all. The pastor was aware that all excessiveness and all aberrant behavior have roots in childhood experiences, and that these events are usually buried. She was sent to the Burlingame Counseling Center.[4]

At the Center she was introduced to Primal Integration, a process whereby a counselee is enabled to relive the buried traumatic incidents of childhood.

"Do you use hypnosis or drugs?" she asked.

"No, you are simply shown how to go back into your early years and relive primal hurts by a unique process of breathing. Each person requires a somewhat different approach."

Reliving Primal Hurts

With some understandable trepidation Sheila lay down on a foam rubber mat in a dimly lit room. Within less than half-an-hour she had learned how to let a portion of her mind drift back to childhood. Hour by hour she relieved primal incidents which had left psychic scars on her personality. There was the deprivation of love, primal fears which were brushed aside by parents, failure to be held and cuddled, nameless anxieties which she learned as a child not to talk about.

In her case, there was no single big traumatic event which created the enormous, diffused anxiety she experienced as an adult. It had simply been the accumulation of scores of ancient hurts which laid the foundation for a deep anxiety neurosis. Her drinking to excess was simply her way of relieving the tension. Her sexual permissiveness was an unconscious effort to get some of the love denied her as a child.

She wrote a few weeks after returning home: "Day by day the positive results of my primal sessions have shown through in my attitudes, acceptance of others, and a greater tolerance. I am grateful to God for the ministry of Primal Integration. Last week a seriously disturbed girl attacked me physically. I discussed this with my minister, and we both agreed that the calm control I was able to use in the encounter was directly attributable to my time there at the Burlingame Counseling Center.

"I have no difficulty with drinking now. It's hard to believe how dependent I had become on booze, and how different my life style is now. Things are going great! Never before have I had so many challenges to face, but never have I experienced so much strength with which to handle them. And I am experiencing a joy in living which I never had before."

She went on to say that her former compulsion to seek sexual encounters outside of marriage had disappeared, and her relationships with everyone around her had changed to a fantastic degree.

Nothing Is Ever Forgotten

Everything that has ever happened to us is inscribed somewhere in the memory bank. Though the event may have transpired many years ago, the memory is lodged somewhere in those fifteen billion cells in the brain. Time does not diminish them in the slightest. The fact that most of the traumas of childhood are "forgotten" does not mean that they are doing no damage. Deep in the unconscious mind they can become festering pools of pain, producing anxiety, tension, character distortion, obsessive-compulsive behavior, alcoholism, drug addiction, difficulty in giving or receiving love, impaired relationships and, in time, actual physical symptoms of a hundred different varieties.

Sigmund Freud wrote of the timelessness of memory: "We have found by experience that unconscious mental processes are in themselves timeless. That is to say . . . they are not arranged in chronological order; time alters nothing in them, nor can the idea of time be applied to them."[5]

A person reliving primal hurts may leap from an event at age three, go back to the crib, then experience something at the age of five. The memories seem to be arranged by subject matter rather than chronologically. That is, a person may be experiencing intense loneliness in the crib and need mother's attention. A bit later there rises the buried memory of painful feelings of loneliness in a new school situation. An astonishing number of "forgotten" instances of sexual molestation are relieved in Primal Integration.

The reliving of forgotten childhood experiences which were painful discharges the anxiety which encapsulates them. As Freud has pointed out, "Repression demands a continuous expenditure of effort."[6] That is, it requires psychic energy to hold those buried feelings and memories down in the unconscious mind. It is believed by many psychiatrists that as much as 50 to 75 percent of a person's psychic energy may be expended in an effort to keep those feelings out of conscious awareness.

Rummaging around in the basement one day, I discovered an ancient Victrola record, "Over There," dated 1918. It was nearly sixty-years-old. I put it on my record prayer and played it, at the old speed of 78 of course, and listened to the ancient strains of a World War I song. It was a bit scratchy from rough handling, but except for that, just as clear and distinct as the day it was made. Time had not affected it. It is the same way with buried memories —they are not affected by time.

Reliving the Past

"Dr. Wilder Penfield, a neurosurgeon, discovered in 1951 incontrovertable evidence that nothing is ever completely forgotten. During brain surgery Penfield used a weak electric current transmitted through a probe to touch the temporal cortex of the brain of a patient. Penfield discovered some amazing and fascinating things during the course of that and subsequent operations. He found that by touching the electric probe to certain portions of the brain the patient could . . . become suddenly aware of a whole series of childhood events and experiences. The patient not only remembered, but more important, relived those events with startling clarity. He heard someone singing a song . . . clearly, and when the electric probe touched another spot the patient said, 'Something brings back a memory. I can see . . . Harrison's Bakery.' At another time the patient heard a popular song being played by an orchestra. At other times the patient hummed a tune along with what was being heard.

"Penfield reports, 'The subject feels again the emotion which the situation originally produced in him, and he is aware of the same interpretation, true or false, which he himself gave to the experience in the first place.' "[7]

After some thousands of hours of listening to persons reliving their painful buried memories, the therapists at the Burlingame Counseling Center report: "For most people talk therapy is largely a waste of time compared to the results obtained with Primal Integration. We have dealt with a vast number of people who have spent years trying to get relief by talking about it, who, in a few weeks of Primal Integration, are able to discharge the accumulated anxiety which had left them less than whole persons."

A great many people report, "But I had a good childhood. I can't remember anything particularly bad about those early years. My parents loved me." Some who have only pleasant memories of childhood often relive under Primal Integration forgotten experiences which were terribly destructive. A fifty-year-old man spent several hours crying. He was in the crib and could see his mother in another room. He needed her desperately. He was lonely and frightened and wanted to be held and loved. That she didn't come meant to the child that he was unloved. Finally in a voice filled with despair he said, "She's never coming. Never. I'll never ask for anything again." And he didn't. He never again asked for love or help, nor expected it.

A Self-fulfilling Prophecy

A former minister who had failed at virtually everything he had undertaken came to understand the reason for his failure. At one point in his primal experience, when he was trying to get love from his unfeeling mother, he said in a conspiratorial voice, "I know what I'll do. I'll fail! That's what I'll do. That'll show her. I'll get back at her. She wants me to succeed, but I'll fail. She can't control me then. I'll be good on the outside, but on the inside I'll rebel and fail. She'll never know why I failed!" He went on for an hour or more plotting the ways he would use to defeat his controlling mother. He had no conscious memory of that tragic life-scarring decision.

W. V. Caldwell writes, "Within our own consciousness, waiting to be recalled, is a memory of every moment, every feeling, every desire in our lives. Nothing is lost, nothing really forgotten, nothing destroyed in the erosion of the years. It means that 'everything survives,' not just intellectually, but in a more complete way, to be refelt, relived, known in fullest colors and emotional intensity. In us the child who played hooky . . . in us the infant screaming for its bottle, in us the agony of being born; in us the silence of mother's womb." [8]

In this connection it is interesting to note that some people who have had a particularly difficult birth go back in Primal Integration and relive the experience, thus discharging the pain and terror which have been encapsulated. It takes enormous energy to keep those memories buried and out of consciousness.

Therapists at the Burlingame Counceling Center report that as of the present time, something over a hundred persons from other states have visited the Center for therapy, including many from the Midwest and East Coast. There is no way to predict how long Primal Integration will require since each person is radically different; but most people spend four hours a day in therapy, for three to four weeks. Local people often devote only two hours a week. Some are able to continue primaling on their own afterwards.

At a retreat which I was conducting, we had broken up into small groups of about a dozen. I was seated next to a woman in her fifties. She was sharing something which seemed rather innocuous, but I noted a catch in her voice, and asked, "What are you feeling?"

"I don't know. Suddenly I just felt like crying."

"Do you want to try to discover what it is?"

"Yes, I think so. It feels like something very old, very painful, from childhood."

I asked her to close her eyes and helped her to relax. Then I had her do some deep breathing and regressed her to childhood.

Suddenly the tears began to flow, and she sobbed uncontrollably. She was encouraged to cry it out, to let herself feel it fully, which she did, completely oblivious of the others in the room. She was back in her childhood reliving some very traumatic events. She talked about it with intense feeling as she reexperienced it.

Her mother had died when she was six. For two years she lived with her grandparents, and then her father farmed her out to an aunt who had eleven other children. "Daddy abandoned me," she said.

Life with the unloving aunt and uncle proved to be a nightmare. Her uncle tried to rape her when she was fourteen, and when she told her aunt she was told, "You led him on! It's all your fault." Then the aunt beat her with a board until her back was raw and bleeding.

Those tragic events had been totally buried. She had absolutely no conscious memory of the attempted rape or the beating, though she had been fourteen years old when it happened.

During her session she expressed hurt and anger toward her father who, she felt, had abandoned her to an unloving aunt and uncle. Then, as she talked about it later, she saw for the first time a connection between the attempted rape, the beating and her sexual frigidity.

Most people have not experienced anything as traumatic as that. A majority of individuals undergoing this type of therapy simply relive the need to be listened to, to be loved and held and cuddled, to feel important. It is terrifying for children to have their parents express anger at them. It is usually not permissible for children to express their anger, or even their hurt. So, they "shut down" and repress the feeling, which drives the pain into the unconscious mind, out of conscious awareness. It is as if a fuse were blown. The child then has no alternative but to become an unfeeling person; his feelings become distorted in some neurotic way.

Someone asked if there is biblical authority for the use of such methods of healing. The response given was, "Yes, it's right there after the passage that authorizes the use of pipe organs in church, and just before the passage which authorizes the removal of a tumor by surgery."

Jesus, we read, "healed all who came." He felt limitless compassion for all who hurt in body, mind or spirit. He commanded his disciples to heal the sick and cleanse the lepers. But he did not tell them how to do it! We do not know how to heal the sick with a touch as Jesus did, but we can help them with modern medical techniques and miracle drugs. Such techniques are providing healing for many people who, a few years ago, would have died. I have a strong conviction that Christ would have us heal the sick and the hurting by *whatever means available*—whether by the laying on of hands by a faith healer, or modern scientific means, by adopting a better diet, proper exercise, surgery, prayer or any method which seems appropriate.

William James, the famous Harvard psychologist, coined the term *pragmatism*. In its simplest form this is the idea that the true test of anything is whether or not it *works*. When John the Baptist sent emissaries to Jesus to ask if he were the promised one, Jesus gave a very pragmatic answer. He said, "Go and tell John what you have seen and heard: the blind receive their sight, the lame walk, lepers are cleansed, and the deaf hear, the dead are raised up, the poor have good news preached to them." [9]

The acid test of the efficacy of any means for achieving wholeness should be found in the results it produces. Don't quarrel with the method. Test the fruits, for "You will know them by their fruits." [10]

Appendix

This psychological test, to indicate the degree of INTEGRATION (Wholeness), is as accurate as you are able to give honest responses to the statements. When you have finished circling your responses, either *True* or *False,* turn the page upside down and read scoring instructions.

True	*False*	1.	My mother gave me lots of love when I was small.
True	*False*	2.	I have a strong religious faith.
True	*False*	3.	I have no serious physical complaints.
True	*False*	4.	I have plenty of friends.
True	*False*	5.	I believe in life after death.
True	*False*	6.	I feel fulfilled most of the time.
True	*False*	7.	Most people can be trusted.
True	*False*	8.	I would like to have the will of God in my life.
True	*False*	9.	My friends seem to let me down.
True	*False*	10.	I have little or no difficulty giving compliments.
True	*False*	11.	Most of the time I am reasonably happy.
True	*False*	12.	I feel people are usually sincere when they compliment me.
True	*False*	13.	I felt loved by my father as a child.
True	*False*	14.	I am basically a very optimistic person.
True	*False*	15.	I have never had periods of deep depression.
True	*False*	16.	I was not punished severely as a child.
True	*False*	17.	I seldom, if ever, feel hopeless about myself.
True	*False*	18.	I have no difficulty giving and receiving love.
True	*False*	19.	I enjoy being with people.
True	*False*	20.	My goals in life are pretty well established.
True	*False*	21.	I very seldom feel tense and anxious.
True	*False*	22.	I have never done things which I think are unforgivable.
True	*False*	23.	I seldom feel inferior to others.
True	*False*	24.	People tend to accept me quite readily.
True	*False*	25.	I don't mind being alone part of the time.
True	*False*	26.	I find it fairly easy to forgive slights and hurts.

Scoring Instructions: Count the number of *TRUE*'s circled. If 20 or above —Splendid Integration, a sense of Wholeness; if 15–20—Good Integration; if 10–15—In need of additional growth; if 1–10—Additional therapy indicated.

Notes

Preface

1. Lane Adams, *How Come It's Taking Me So Long To Get Better?* (Wheaton, Illinois: Tyndale House Publishers, Inc., 1975).
2. Rom. 7:18, LB.
3. 1 Tim. 1:15, RSV.
4. Matt. 15:33, NEB.
5. Mark 14:66–70, NEB.
6. 1 Cor. 5:1, RSV.
7. 2 Cor. 1:8, RSV.
8. Eph. 4:31, RSV.
9. *Eclectic:* Choosing what appears to be the best from diverse sources, systems, styles or methods; from the Greek *eklektikos,* to single out.

Chapter 1: Are You a Whole Person?

1. Quoted by Ernest Becker in *Denial of Death* (New York: The Free Press, a division of Macmillan Publishing Co., 1975).
2. Acts 11:9–29, RSV.
3. Gen. 12:10–20; 20:2–7, RSV.
4. Num. 20:1–13, RSV.
5. 1 Kings: 19:1–14, RSV.
6. 1 Kings 11:1–8, RSV.
7. Max Lerner, "The Real Mr. America," *Quest,* March/April 1977.
8. Isa. 53:6, RSV.
9. Acts 20:35, RSV.
10. Matt. 5:42, RSV.
11. *Psychology Newsletter,* July 1975.

Chapter 2: Wholeness and Childhood

1. *Human Behavior,* July 1976.
2. W. V. Caldwell, *Psycholytic Therapy* (New York: Grove Press, 1968).
3. Ibid.
4. Ibid.
5. Karen Horney, M.D., *Neurosis and Human Growth* (New York: W. W. Norton and Co., 1950).
6. Ibid.
7. Soren Kierkegaard, *Sickness Unto Death* (Princeton University Press).
8. Karen Horney, M.D. *Neurosis and Human Growth* (New York: W. W. Norton and Co., 1950).
9. W. V. Caldwell, *Psycholytic Therapy* (New York: Grove Press, 1968).

Chapter 3: Serenity, Stress and Anxiety
1. Available from Yokefellows, Inc., 19 Park Road, Burlingame, California 94010.
2. Luke 6:38, RSV.
3. John 16:33, RSV.
4. Hans Selye, M.D., *Stress Without Distress* (New York: J. B. Lippincott Co., 1974).
5. Ibid.

Chapter 4: Religion and Wholeness
1. Vernon Grounds, Ph.D., *Emotional Problems and the Gospel* (Michigan: Zondervan Publishing Co., 1976).
2. Ibid.
3. Carl Michalson, *Faith for Personal Crises* (New York: Charles Scribner's Sons, 1958).
4. Martin Marty, in *Time,* October 27, 1975.
5. Ibid.
6. Rev. 11:15, LB.
7. Eli Chesen, M.D., *Religion May Be Hazardous to Your Health* (Collier Books, 1973).
8. The Burlingame Counseling Center, 19 Park Road, Burlingame, California 94010.
9. John 14:1, RSV.

Chapter 5: Are You a Neurotic?
1. Rom. 3:23, NEB.
2. Virginia Satir, *Peoplemaking* (Palo Alto, California: Science and Behavior Books, 1975).

Chapter 6: Love, Marriage and Wholeness
1. Anthony Storr, *Human Aggression* (New York: Bantam Books, 1968).
2. Matt. 23:23, NEB.
3. Judith Vorst, *Redbook,* February 1975.
4. *The San Francisco Chronicle,* February 10, 1977.
5. Anthony Storr, *Human Aggression* (New York: Bantam Books, 1968).
6. Burlingame Counseling Center, 19 Park Road, Burlingame, California 94010.
7. W. W. Broadbent, M.D., *How To Be Loved* (Englewood Cliffs, New Jersey: Prentice Hall, 1976).
8. Daniel Casriel, M.D., *A Scream Away from Happiness* (New York: Grossett and Dunlap Publishers, 1972).
9. Discussed in more detail in Chapter 14.

Chapter 7: Aging, Death and Immortality
1. Robert Browning, "Pippa Passes."

2. Hokusai, "A Hundred Views of Fuji" *Encyclopedia of World Art* (McGraw-Hill, 1963), Vol. 7, Column 584.
3. Alex Comfort, *A Good Age* (New York: Crown Publishers, 1976).
4. Charlie Brower, *Me and Other Advertising Geniuses* (New York: Doubleday).
5. Daniel Goleman, "We Are Breaking the Silence About Death," *Psychology Today*, September 1976.

   For more information read: Chicago: Glaser, Barney G. and Anself L. Strauss, *Awareness of Dying*, (Chicago: Aldine Publishing Co., 1965).; Kapleau, Philip, *The Wheel of Death*, (New York: Harper & Row, 1974).; Kübler-Ross, Elisabeth, ed. *Death: The Final Stage of Growth*, (New York: Prentice-Hall, 1975).; Kübler-Ross, Elisabeth, *On Death and Dying*, (New York: Macmillan Publishing Co., Inc., 1969).; Shneidman, Edwin S., ed. *Death: Current Perspectives*, (Palo Alto, Calif.: Mayfield Publishing Co., 1976).

   An album of five cassettes by Elisabeth Kübler–Ross, reviewing and summarizing her experiences with the needs of terminally ill patients and their families, is available from the *Psychology Today Library Cassettes*. Write to: Ross Cassettes, Consumer Service Division, 595 Broadway, New York, NY 10012.
6. *Family Circle*, September 1975.
7. Ibid.
8. Raynor Johnson, *The Imprisoned Splendour* (New York: Harper & Row, 1953).
9. Raymond A. Moody, *Life After Life* (Covington, Georgia: Mockingbird Books, 1975).
10. Luke 16:31, RSV.
11. 1 Cor. 15:4–7, RSV.
12. Quoted by Jung in *Jung: And the Story of Our Time* by Laurens van der Post (New York: Pantheon Books, Random House Publishers, 1975).
13. Ibid.
14. Ibid.
15. Bernard de Champillon
16. John 3:12, NEB.
17. *California Living Magazine*, January 30, 1977.
18. Norman Vincent Peale, "Why I Believe in Life After Life," *Guideposts*, April 1977.
19. John 15:9, 10, NEB.

Chapter 8: Self-Esteem and Wholeness

1. Laurens van der Post, *Jung: And the Story of Our Time* (New York: Pantheon Books, Random House Publishers, 1975).
2. Matt. 18:6, 7, NEB.
3. John 10:34, RSV.
4. Hans Selye, M.D., *Stress Without Distress* (New York: J. B. Lippincott Co., 1974).

5. Ernest Becker, *The Denial of Death* (New York: The Free Press, a division of Macmillan Publishing Co., 1975).
6. T. S. Eliot, *The Cocktail Party* (New York: Harcourt Brace & Co., 1950).
7. Matt. 5, 6, and 7, RSV.
8. Luke 6:38, RSV.
9. Matt. 5:44, RSV.
10. Luke 11:9, RSV.
11. Gal. 5:22, NEB.

Chapter 9: Guilt and Wholeness
1. Rom. 3:23, NEB.
2. Laurens van der Post, *Jung: And the Story of Our Time* (New York: Pantheon Books, Random House Publishers, 1975).
3. Sigmund Freud, *Dictionary of Psychoanalysis* (Connecticut: Fawcett Publications, Inc., 1958).
4. Rom. 7:18, LB.
5. Acts 13:22, 23, LB.
6. Deut. 4:29, RSV.

Chapter 10: Life Isn't Fair
1. Sheldon B. Kopp, *If You Meet the Buddha on the Road, Kill Him* (Ben Lomond, California: Science and Behavior Books, 1972).
2. John 16:33, RSV.
3. Rev. 21:4, RSV.
4. Matt. 7:7, RSV.
5. Phil. 2:13, NEB.
6. Gen. 1:26, RSV.
7. John 12:31, 14:30, 16:11, RSV.
8. Eph. 2:2, RSV.
9. Estimate by a commission of the United Nations.
10. Rom. 5:3, RSV.
11. Matt. 18:14, RSV.
12. Leslie D. Weatherhead, *The Will of God* (Nashville: Abingdon Press, 1944).
13. Rev. 11:15, RSV.

Chapter 11: Fear, Anxiety and Wholeness
1. 1 John 4:18, RSV.
2. Paul Tournier, *The Whole Person in a Broken World* (New York: Harper & Row, 1964).
3. Luke 16:13, RSV.
4. John 8:31, 32, RSV.
5. Philip Zimbardo, Robert M. Norwood and Paul A. Pilkonis, "The Social Disease Called Shyness," *Psychology Today*, May 1975.

Chapter 12: Do You Really Want to Be a Whole Person?
1. John 1:1-4, NEB.

124405

2. Matt. 9:20, RSV.
3. Karl Menninger, *The Crime of Punishment* (New York: The Viking Press, 1976).
4. Hans Selye, M.D., *Stress Without Distress* (New York: J. B. Lippincott Co., 1974).
5. John 7:17, NEB.
6. Deut. 4:29, RSV.

Chapter 13: Paths to Wholeness
1. Jerome Frank, *Persuasion and Healing: A Comparative Study of Psychotherapy* (Baltimore, Maryland: Johns Hopkins Press, 1961).
2. Thomas C. Oden, *Game Free: A Guide to the Meaning of Intimacy* (New York: Harper & Row, 1974).
3. Burlingame Counseling Center, 19 Park Road, Burlingame, California 94010.
4. Thomas A. Harris, *I'm OK–You're OK* (New York: Avon Publishing, 1973).
5. Ibid.
6. Matt. 16:18, NEB.
7. John 13:35, RSV.
8. *Webster's New Collegiate Dictionary.*
9. 1 Cor. 14:18, RSV.
10. 1 Cor. 14:5, RSV.
11. Ibid.
12. Dennis and Rita Bennett, *The Holy Spirit and You* (New Jersey: Logos International, 1973).
13. Mark 7:24–30, RSV.

Chapter 14: More Paths to Wholeness
1. Herbert Benson, M.D., *The Relaxation Response* (New York: Avon Publishing, 1976).
2. Arthur Janov, Ph.D., *The Primal Scream* (New York: Dell Publishing, 1970).
3. Arthur Janov, Ph.D., *The Primal Revolution* (New York: Simon & Schuster, 1972).
4. Associated with Yokefellows, Inc., 19 Park Road, Burlingame, California 94010.
5. Sigmund Freud, *Dictionary of Psychoanalysis* (Connecticut: Fawcett Publications Inc., 1958).
6. Ibid.
7. W. Penfield, "Memory Mechanisms," American Medical Association, Archives of Neurology and Psychiatry, 1952.
8. W. V. Caldwell, *Psycholytic Therapy* (New York: Grove Press, 1968).
9. Luke 7:22, RSV.
10. Matt. 7:16, RSV.